THE SECRET ART OF HAPPINESS:

Change Your Life with the Reiki Ideals

By Geneva Robins

koeus studios

THE SECRET ART OF HAPPINESS:

Change Your Life with the Reiki Ideals

ISBN: 978-0-9953040-0-0

Published in 2016

Published by Koeus Studios Inc. Calgary. AB, Canada

Printed by CreateSpace, Charleston SC, USA

Also Available on Kindle and other devices

Foreword — Master Usui

The creative impulse is the throb of life. It elevates everything to the sublime. It transforms daily drudgery to magical shining moments. Creativity is the basis of happiness. Bringing forth the magic and mystery of the human experience, in the way only *you* can, is a Divine calling. It uplifts and transforms everything.

Your creativity, your good works upon the Earth, gets blocked by fear, doubt, anger, worry, and unhappiness. You are hindered in your ability to create real meaning and change in your life as long as these disturbing emotions are given free reign over your daily experience.

Happiness is generated from within. Happiness is no accident. It is the result of deliberately letting go of undesirable conditions (anger and worry) and cultivating desirable conditions (gratitude, meditative focus, and kindness). Happiness allows you to access greater levels of abundance, creativity, and generosity than you have ever experienced. True and deep transformation of the self and the world is possible when you are willing to wrestle with the causes of unhappiness and root them out.

The constriction caused by tough times is a bottleneck in your personal evolution. You differentiate and grow in new and wondrous ways. Here, on the other side, we (all of us non-physical ones) are constantly amazed and surprised by your ingenuity when you allow the solution to your struggle to flow in. From our position, we could not create in the way you do, because our diversity of experience is not as great. Your solutions are unique in the Universe.

So to receive what you want, be it happiness, wealth, relationships, or a basket of kittens, you need to let go a bit and trust that the answer appears on **this** side, the instant you have that need, want, or desire. We, your guides and helpers, instantly know the solution **you** have created, and if you let us, we will guide you toward your desire.

Your guides are the intercessors between Divine, Creative Energy and your intention. The more you listen to your intuition and guidance, the more of your creations become manifest in your life.

Your creativity and your art are unique in the world. Only **you** can bring them into the world the way **you** can. The beauty of creative projects is that the world craves them and wants more and more of them.

Do not get talked out of your dream by well-meaning people. **Trust** in your ability to do the impossible. Believe you can, and the world will yield even greater manifestations.

The world needs **you**. The world needs your contribution. The entire universe is waiting to yield to you all you desire. It is yours. You need only ask. Put in the small time and tiny effort, daily, to increase your happiness, and you will uplift the **entire** world.

~ Mikao Usui, as channelled by Geneva Robins

Table of Contents

CHAPTER ONE:

Introduction

The breezes at dawn
Have secrets to tell you.
Don't go back to sleep!
   ~ Rumi

About Me and This Book

This book started with the click of a pen.

Actually, it was a persistent clicka-clicka-clicka noise that woke me up in the pre-dawn hours of a spring day in 2014. My son had crawled into bed with us for the usual morning cuddle, but instead of playing games on my phone or pretending to sleep like he normally does, he had found a pen.

Clicka-clicka-clicka.

I should let you know I had been receiving 'pen' messages from multiple sources over the months leading up to the morning with all the clicking, but I had neatly ignored them. I *knew* I wanted to write a book about my experiences teaching Reiki *someday*, but I didn't feel ready. I was delaying, avoiding, hiding.

I *knew* I had created something magical in my courses, something beyond me, something changing lives before my eyes.

I had opened up and channelled the information for the courses, and people were recovering from addictions, healing depression, and suicide ideation, and accessing depths of happiness that were stable, resilient, and real. I knew I had to find a way to bring this work to a larger audience, to people who might not know about Reiki or have any interest in learning it. There were fundamental lessons within the material that were innately transformative. There was a book in me. I *knew* it. Someday.

I might have stayed there, teaching comfortably small classes in the comfort of my friend's living room. Hiding. But I had enough experience with the consequences of not following my Dharma, my life path and purpose, to know that, sooner or later, I would need to cast off the last of the smallness and really be who I am.

This is the occupational hazard of people who teach others transformational work; they must also transform. I teach others to follow their own good advice and to embrace their 'bigness', and now, I was being called to do the same.

Clicka-clicka-clicka.

That you're reading this at all means you know how that morning played out. I rose from bed. I did not go back to sleep. I listened to the ancient Rumi poem, quivering in the morning stillness, echoing in my brain, and I wrote. I wrote for hours. I wrote not clearly knowing what I was to write, but just that I **must** write. I only needed to show up, and the Divine calling me to the page would do the rest. That was the deal. I got out of the way. The Divine showed up. I wrote.

The book that has emerged from that process of surrender has changed me more than I can say. The wisdom that wrote itself on the page taught me to love my body (once and for all), to trust my ability to channel the Divine, and to really *know* that I cannot hide this material from the world to preserve my timid ego. I can help. This I know.

The material in this book works. I know this because it worked for me, and it is working for my students. This stuff I teach heals and transforms lives. It creates happiness. It dissolves fear and worry and anger. It boosts worthiness and faith and kindness. It is gratitude creating more gratitude. Love creating more love. It is magic.

"This is the moment where sh#t gets real." I tell my students. This is the kind of book that requires doing, rolling up your metaphorical sleeves and getting to work. It is not a gathering-dust-on-the-shelf book. It is a workbook in the truest sense of the word. You must do the work.

The work is not hard, but it may not always be easy. The work is fun, though you might sometimes resist it. The work is gentle, but you might not always like it.

It works.

Try. Do. Change.

Clicka-clicka-clicka

Master Usui, Me, and Instant Messaging the Universe

Master Mikao Usui was the founder of Reiki and is my ever present spiritual guide. He lived in Japan from 1860 to 1925 and created the Usui Shiki Ryoho System of Natural Healing. I learned to channel his clear guidance after a series of experiences that opened up my connection to the divine. Mainly, I had to develop the needed desire to contact him, the belief I could do it, and the knowing that I was worthy to receive his wisdom directly.

I had several "getting out of the way" experiences that made it possible to fully acknowledge my skill in communicating with non-physical beings. Up till then, I had sporadic communications with the spirit world, but nothing so clear and consistent as I experience now.

Now, it is like switching the channel or writing an email and getting an instant reply. Hmm, maybe not email, but instant messaging? Yes, that is it, I can now IM any non-physical being in the universe and get a clear reply. This is how I was able to write much of this book.

I began to develop the ability to get out of the way while writing when I was finishing up my Master's thesis in ecology in 2009. I had a hard deadline to finish my thesis by a certain date or I would not pass. I was able to write a 365-page manuscript in about six weeks. I dutifully showed up at the page and got myself completely out of the way. Even though the writing was scientific, technical writing, I would sit in the coffee shop, open my laptop, and say "Hit it, God!" I would then write sentence after sentence, until I needed to go home to nurse my 9-month old son. Quite the way to finish a hard science manuscript! But finish, I did. And quite well too. It all taught me to stand aside and let the words flow.

Getting out of the way in **all** of my writing had then become the norm for me after finishing my thesis. It all flowed naturally. It was the easiest way for me to set aside all worry, all fear, all apprehension, and just allow what was needed to be written to be written. It was an easy extension to begin to ask direct questions of spiritual beings that I trusted for the advice I needed.

I began channelling during my writing sessions in 2012, after a series of family tragedies rocked me to my foundations. Two very dear family members died within two weeks of each other. It was devastating. Days later, I learned my niece would require open heart surgery, my son caught a severe stomach virus, and my husband got kidney stones. It was a very turbulent time, and I did my best to reach for the light in the midst of so much despair.

I began, at first, writing questions to Abraham, a group of entities that the amazing Esther Hicks channels as part of their *Law of Attraction* books and workshops. I had a thirst to understand why these terribly sad circumstances were happening all at once and how I was to ever get out from underneath the mountain of grief that laid in their wake. I would write down a question troubling me and then write the response I *'heard'* in my mind or Inner Ear. I would record the information as faithfully as I could, trying my best not to alter a single word or phrase as it appeared in my mind.

I gained a great deal of solace and insight into the purpose of these difficult times. By just talking to these wise ones on the other side, I felt relief. Soon I wrote to my departed loved ones, and their responses soothed the deep pain and grief overwhelming my heart. They were not gone. Not even a little. They were more full, more vibrant, more alive than ever. They were still there! They are still here, now, cheering me on as I write these words, encouraging me to get past my nervousness about exposing this private part of my life that is admittedly a little weird. Or, maybe a lot weird!

It took a little while to realize that, if I could channel my departed loved ones, then I could channel any being that was non-physical. I did not have to wait; I could talk to any of them, to all of them. I began writing to Master Usui, and he immediately came through loud and clear. The advice was always neat, to the point, and immeasurably helpful. He guided me in creating my Reiki courses. Together, the format of the classes expanded from what I was originally taught by my teachers to incorporate all of the current information in mind-body medicine with the traditional Reiki teachings.

Reiki used to be taught over years, but today, it is most often learned over the course of two weekends. I compromised and developed 4 eight week courses, which allow my students to reach the Master level in one year. Master Usui very clearly guided the material and meditations in the courses. The result was a series of courses that not only taught people Reiki, but also began to heal their lives significantly. I began to ask myself how I could share the magic of the courses with a wider audience.

What was it within the courses that was allowing people the opportunity to transform their pain into wisdom? I looked for similarities in the people getting the greatest success. What they shared in common, besides a firm resolve to change, was that they all applied the Reiki Ideals to their daily lives. When I taught them about the Ideals, they didn't just parrot the words. They really dug into the meaning of each Ideal and started living them. The Reiki Ideals are also called the 'Secret Art of Inviting Happiness'. The people who approached the Ideals as instructions for happiness became happy. It was magically simple, but it worked.

This book arose from that same magic. Channelling the wisdom from Master Usui was a huge part of how this book was created. The material presented here came through so clearly that I could feel the transformation within me as I wrote. It was like I was literally writing this new information down into my very DNA, right down to the essence of me.

Not only did I get a book out of the deal, but I also learned, once more, the invaluable resource of practice. Just returning to the same simple practice, every day — that alone will change your life. Just a teeny, tiny commitment to meditate, to change your thoughts, to practice gratitude — these tiny actions add up. Actually, they more than add up; they grow exponentially. You get bigger and bigger rewards the longer you practice anything. Learning a new way to approach your happiness is no different. Practice makes you happy.

How YOU can Work with Master Usui

Master Usui can help you too as you read this book. Whether you have been attuned to Reiki or not, Master Usui helps all who ask. But first, you must ask!

Master Usui is an ascended master, and just like Jesus, Buddha, or Ganesh, can be called upon by anyone for help with any problem. Master Usui specializes in healing, but also with calming anger and worry, increasing patience, providing clear guidance on your next steps in life, and inviting happiness into your daily experience.

Usui's goal in working with you is to uplift you on every level, spiritually, mentally, emotionally, and physically. He can direct you in the actions and thoughts that will speed your healing. He will give you Reiki or support your Reiki practice. If you already know and use Reiki, or even teach it, he will boost your healing abilities and give you insight on how the Reiki energy works and specific information you can share to help your clients and students.

As you go through the material in this book, you can call upon Master Usui's loving presence to guide you through *any* challenges you might face in *any* area of your life.

Master Usui loves helping all who call upon him, but just like other ascended masters, he cannot intervene in your life unasked. You must ask! Permission is key in Reiki. He is unable to help you unless you ask, and you must ask every single time. He arrives instantly when called, but you must call.

Asking for Usui's help can be as simple as just thinking the thought, "Master Usui, please come help me with..." He shows up right away and gets to work. As with all the other spiritual masters, the more you get out of the way, the easier it is for them to do their job.

It is a lot like calling an ambulance; first, you must call for help and describe the problem. Next, you allow them to arrive.

Then, you stand back and let them do their work. Just as you would not tell a paramedic how to set up an IV, you also don't need to direct Master Usui on how to best heal you. He's got it! You *do* need to get out of the way. The more you can relax and follow the flow of the energy and the guidance you're receiving, the better able Master Usui can help you.

Reiki, my Work, and Healing

Reiki is very old. The system of Reiki may have only originated a mere 120 years ago by Mikao Usui in Japan, but it is based upon a system of energy healing and enlightenment practises that reach back centuries to the time of the Buddha.

Energy healing itself has existed for as long as there have been people. Many cultures and faiths throughout the world discuss the ability of certain people to heal by the laying on of hands.

Everyone possesses the ability to heal. Heal both themselves and heal others. What the system of Reiki allows for is the easy training and guidance to access this natural ability, expand it, and bring clear focus to the Divine healing energy available to us all. Reiki tunes us up to become natural conduits of the same energy that can grow a tree, cause a cell to divide, a baby to be born, or a bone to heal.

This natural energy force, we call Reiki, travels through the body of the practitioner and through their hands to the recipient, the one being healed. The energy is not coming *from* the practitioner, but *through* them. The Attunement process of Reiki allows this Divine energy to pass through the practitioner cleanly. The healing meditations and inner work the Reiki practitioner does daily keeps this channel open and at a high vibration.

Most of my work in teaching is to assist my students in letting go of resistance in all forms in their lives. By letting go of resistance, the Reiki work they do is much more effective, both for the work they do with others and the personal, self-healing work they do on their own.

By taking it slowly, my students not only learn Reiki, but transform their whole lives. They become happy, truly happy, in a way they have never experienced before. They are able to weather the inevitable storms of life, with much more ease and courage than they ever knew they contained. It has blossomed into a deeply healing, personal journey of growth and development.

Reiki is a spiritual discipline. It requires dedication. It requires a practitioner to do their own self-healing work, **before** they consider helping others. It does not require us, as practitioners or teachers, to be perfect, but it does require us to continually and steadily increase our own levels of happiness, patience, and understanding. As I often tell my students, "I'm not perfect, but the work is!" If you do the work, the real inner, self-healing work, the result is perfect.

Reiki is traditionally, and properly, taught by receiving a series of Attunements from a Master. Reiki **cannot** be learned in a book. Be wary of anyone who tells you otherwise. To harness the true power and complexity of Reiki for maximum benefit, find a **great** teacher.

This book **will not** teach you Reiki. For that, you need to get yourself a Master Teacher.

This book **will**, however, teach you to access your own self-healing abilities, increase your powers of focus and attention, and to use the wisdom within the Reiki Ideals to change your life substantially and tangibly. Read this book, do the work, and I assure you, happiness will no longer be a secret.

Reiki Ideals

The Reiki Ideals are five very simple principles that guide a person toward happiness. Master Usui adopted them from the Mei-ji emperor and incorporated them into the Reiki system. They provide a basic philosophy of living a great life and are often called the 'secret art of inviting happiness'. They are called this for a reason; they work.

When my students really incorporated the Reiki Ideals into their lives, they changed so profoundly that they were almost different people from week to week. The anger, worry, criticism, worthlessness, and cruelty that might have plagued them before were gradually replaced with peace, faith, gratitude, worthiness, and kindness. They were happier than they ever remember being.

And I was happier too. I found that living by the Ideals was not always easy, but being aware of these simple concepts shifted longstanding patterns of worry, fear, and anger within me. Happiness stopped being some elusive, out-there, far-away thing to be chased down and attained; it lived within me. I could access it, reliably, with the skills of Reiki and the daily application of the Reiki Ideals throughout my life.

The Reiki Ideals are:

Just for today:
> Do not Anger.
> Do not Worry.
> Be Grateful for your many blessings.
> Do your work (meditation) honestly.
> Be kind to yourself and every living thing.

Simple.

Right! So the first one... How do you do that exactly? Let go of anger? And then after that? Worry? I'm worried that I might not be able to let go of worry.

That is a common response to the Reiki Ideals when I teach, "That's nice, but HOW do I do that, exactly?"

This book is really all about just that, integrating the Reiki Ideals* into daily life, breaking them down into manageable exercises, and getting to happiness.

How to Use this Book

This book is mainly focused on the five Reiki Ideals, with a chapter focusing on each one, but it also goes into some core concepts I teach in my Reiki courses that have been really effective in helping people shift their lives and deal with whatever comes up in a healthy and productive way.

This book teaches you to get happy. It teaches you to resolve anger and worry. It gives you a daily, practical way of recording your many blessings. It helps you build a home

---

* Original Reiki Ideals
The secret art of inviting happiness.
The miraculous medicine of all diseases.
Just for today, do not anger.
Do not worry, and be filled with gratitude.
Devote yourself to your work and be kind to people.
Every morning and evening join your hands in prayer, pray these words to your heart, and chant these words with your mouth.

Modern Reiki Ideals
Just for today, I will let go of anger.
Just for today, I will let go of worry.
Just for today, I will give thanks for my many blessings.
Just for today, I will do my work honestly.
Just for today, I will be kind to my neighbour and every living thing.

Five principles of the Meiji Emperor
From the inscription on Mikao Usui's Memorial Stone:

1) Don't get angry today.
2) Don't worry today.
3) Be grateful today.
4) Work hard today (meditative practise).
5) Be kind to others today.

practise of meditation. It allows you to access the kindness and compassion the Divine feels for all living beings and put it to daily work. It transforms you. This book allows you to be **you**. It allows you to **grow**. It gives you **permission** to change and be happy.

Each of the chapters builds on the next, so while it is tempting to skip around, do try to work it through from start to finish. Just note where you're getting stuck. It is okay. Please do these exercises haphazardly, imperfectly, or not at all. Appreciate your impulse to run and hide, or throw the book in a corner, or not read a section. That is cool. Hey, that is perfectly normal. Who wants to wade through all their issues with anger, worry, criticism, worthlessness, and cruelty?

Ugh! C'mon! Can't there be an easy, fluffy skies and rainbow version? Can't I just skip over all this crap and just get happy?

No. ...and...Yes.

First, if you're able to stay in fluffy skies and rainbow land in the midst of your difficulties, then you don't need this book; you have got it mastered.

Second, being truly happy is not about stuffing down things that bother you and pretending they don't exist; it is about digesting your experiences, releasing your emotions in a productive way, and getting some Divine context for the work you need to do to really access that space of Divine Love consistently.

And lastly, the urge to skip a part, to bail out, to stop and close the book to numb out on TV, food, wine, or chocolate is juicy! It is a juicy, great, and beautiful thing. Because that is when you know you really hit the core of it. That is when you know you're really digging into the places where you stick, where happiness and joy are eluding you. Honour your experience. Honour your resistance. And then pick up the book and do it anyway. Do the exercises and meditations poorly, petulantly, whatever it takes; whatever you feel, just do them. They work.

This book is peppered liberally with meditations* and *Stop and Give Me 5!* moments. Practising meditation is preparation for living a joyous and happy life. Meditation gives you the ability to train and focus your mind on the thoughts of your choosing. These are little reminders to pause, take 5 minutes, and deliberately tune into the Source greater than you.

Oh! Side note! I use the words God, Goddess, The Divine, Source, The Universe, interchangeably. You can choose whichever word resonates the most with you. Ultimately, the divine is unnameable, intangible, and so much bigger than any one word. Please take your pick!

Affirmation work is practise for selecting positive thoughts and shifting your internal dialogue to be consistent with happiness, peace, and love. In the *Affirmation Ladder* sections, I integrate the need for honesty with the desire to change your thoughts. Instead of leaping to a strongly positive affirmation that might feel like a lie, you rate your anger, worry, gratitude, meditative or self-care work, and your kindness on a scale of zero to ten. There is a separate affirmation for each level on the ladder. Basically, you can climb your way up, bit by bit, to some amazingly positive thoughts that will feel true for you.

The *Signs of Spring* journaling exercises will train you to look for all the tiny and miraculous ways your life is changing for the better. Noticing things to appreciate, as little signs of spring, speeds up the shifts in your body, mind and experience, as you begin to notice your positive thoughts and meditative

---

* Check out genevarobins.com/SecretArtMeditations to download free recordings of all the meditations contained within this book. :) You're welcome!

practises are beginning to have a noticeable effect in your life. Gratitude and Appreciation always rev your manifestation engine.

Each chapter has a section devoted to expanding and refining your **Intuition**. Working with and refining your intuition allows you to tap into the immense wisdom of the Divine. Your natural abilities will expand as you practise using your intuition daily. You will get to put your insight and intuition to practical use in improving your life and becoming truly happy.

The *Self Care and Love* sections in each chapter are little nudges to care and love yourself the way God does, with abandon and with great exuberance. Being gentle with yourself as you're making these changes is very important; accepting where you are and loving yourself anyway is a big message here. You don't need to be perfect to get love. God /the Divine/ the Universe loves you as you are in this messy and imperfect moment.

The **Just for Today** sections in each chapter allow you to integrate these changes in a joyful way on a daily basis. It gives you something concrete to do, so you know you can always take inspired action to shift your energy and your body-mind. All of these things together are what makes this book really work for you.

My hope is that the tools, meditations, and activities in this book will help you shift, so you may live a full and vibrant life that is all your own. I see you as happy, fulfilled, and joyous.

And...Go!

CHAPTER TWO:

Intention

We choose our joys and sorrows long before we experience them.
~ **Khalil Gibran**

Intention and the Power of Choice

Everything you have, accomplish, own, or do begins with an intention. Whether it is aloud or not, whether it is known or not, whether it is a conscious choice or a subconscious one, intention is the force that moves energy.

The goal of most self-development work is to make deliberate conscious choices in every aspect of our lives. To choose what we focus our thoughts and feelings on is our true power. Much of our day to day lives are driven by instinctual behaviour and habitual thoughts. We respond without thinking and think without reason, we reason without intuition, and we cloud our deep intuitive impulses with numbing behaviours that drown out the very loud, very persistent calling of our souls.

Setting an intention is similar to picking a target before we draw back the bow and let our arrow fly. We have no guarantee we will reach our target, but if we do not focus and choose, then we **absolutely** won't reach what we want. The archer does not focus on the trees or the ground. Neither should we. An intention is a sole focus on what we want, not what we don't. If you focus on the dirt in front of you, that is all you get!

The absolute best way to set an intention is to first tune into your Inner Being or Higher Self, your soul. This process of turning inward is HUGELY important. Don't skip it. You want the biggest, noblest, most Divine aspect of yourself to have a say in what you focus on. Your Inner Being is wise and can see the wider view of the arc of your whole life, from birth to death. When you tune into that wisdom, the intention you set is also wise. You won't be tempted to manifest surface trinkets that won't bring you lasting happiness. You will be guided to the intention, focus, and target that will bring you lasting contentment that you will feel within the core of your being, long after you leave your physical body.

Turning inward can be as simple as taking a deep breath, a few moments of meditation in a busy day, a stroll in nature, a gaze at the moon and stars in wonder of the mystery.

Quiet times, like these, are when your deep intuitive voice, your soul's voice, can be heard the clearest. That wise voice gives you insight, understanding, and context to your current life situation. It can provide the kind guidance you need to set an intention that is truly wise.

Setting Intention and Getting Out of the Way

An intention is a simple statement that declares your decision to change.

Setting an intention is a step toward getting out of the way. You don't need to know **how** you will get to your happy result; you just need to be **willing** to be taken on that journey — to be *willing* to make the tiny changes, tiny choices that will add up to a *big* difference in your life.

Know that you're the most powerful person in your own life. Know that you're worthy of Divine LOVE and affection. Know that powerful, positive changes *are* happening right NOW as you read this. Know that, as you follow your Soul's voice, you will be guided to a wonderful new *life*. Know that every step on your journey so far has been necessary to get you to this point. Know that your positive intention *can* change your life. Indeed, it can change the whole world.

Mindful Choice and Happiness

Intentions are really just statements that affirm what you want for yourself. The power of setting an intention, besides just knowing where you are going, is because it is a deliberate *choice*. And choices shift *EVERYTHING*!

Consider a time when you took a leisurely stroll through a park in your city or town. You were embracing and experiencing the sights and sounds of Nature and letting her speak to your soul. Now, think about other times you walked in the same park, same conditions, and all you could experience was the drone of your own confused thoughts and feelings.

What made the difference between these two experiences?

A *choice*.

Just a simple decision to listen deeply, beyond the chatter of ego and illusion, and hear the wisdom within.

That difference in experience can occur, no matter what is going on in your life, no matter how many deadlines or busyness your life includes. It can happen the instant you choose to listen to the wise, old soul you really are and let that wisdom guide your life. It happens when you set your sights on your intention to be happy.

Intention can shift everything.

The best intention is a simple, straightforward sentence you can hold steady in your mind. Intentions can also be a word, a phrase, or an image — anything that can anchor you in the energy you're wanting to manifest. A visualization of being happy, healthy, whole, and complete is the best and simplest intention to hold. You can also add to that mental picture any goal you wish to attain of any healing you want to occur. It is important to visualize the result of what you want as already completed. If you really want to move forward in your life, you must surrender the illusion of powerlessness you have had until now. You are powerful.

You are more powerful than you can even imagine. *You*, and you alone, have the power to *completely* shift every aspect of your life. No exceptions. Not one other person needs to understand this, but you in order to change your life experience.

You are powerful. More powerful than you can imagine. I had to write that again. I need to emphasize this point very strongly, because if you get nothing else from this book, know this... YOU ARE POWERFUL!

The entire universe flows in response to decisions. Simple choices, really. Left or right? Blue or orange? Yes or no?

These tiny, daily choices form the basis of our lives. A positive intention hones and focuses these tiny choices into deliberate acts of self-love. Intention allows us to mindfully choose our lives, instead of haphazardly following the flow of other people's decisions.

We focus. We choose. We live. In the process, we find the true source of happiness was within us all along.

An intention is a choice, and all energy flows from a point of decision. The stronger you can hold an intention, the stronger the energy will flow.

Now, to be clear, I am talking about strength the way the ocean is strong; it is only the lowest surface on earth. Or the way the sun is strong, but only runs on a few simple elements and gravity to keep going. Strength, in this context, is not about pushing against anything, but rather, it is a simple point of focus that is held steadily.

The focus that is held is one that is appealing, brings joy, relief, and is in the highest and best interest of all involved. It harms none and helps all. A clear and positive intention brings many wonderful changes and clarity to life.

This is what I mean by intention: A positive uplifting thought about how things could be.

The Observer Effect and Why Your Choices Actually Matter

Every decision you make has a ripple effect on the universe. For reals!

Physicists talk about the superimposition of all possibilities that occurs before a decision has been made. All possibilities exist within the same space and time, until a *choice* determines which possibility will become real.

It baffled many brilliant minds. When they were studying the nature of light in the 1920s, they posed this question in their experiments: Is light a particle or is it a wave? They got different results, depending on their *thoughts* about what was true! Really.

The truth is, light is both. Particle *and* wave. It is probably even weirder than we are led to believe. Weirder than we are able to think.

In studying light and subatomic particles, the building blocks of all matter, physicists found all possibilities can occur in the same time and space *before* the experiment began. The nature of the question *itself* formulated the outcome of the experiment before they even set up their equipment. In physics, this wobbly outcome, based on the attitude and ideas of the experimenter, is called the observer effect.

The *question* generates the answer!

It is the effect of the *observer* that makes things *real!*

As the experiments progressed, the researchers found the same observer effect in electrons. That is matter! Real stuff! Thoughts affect matter!

Mainstream science, for the most part, has left these quantum discoveries locked in the subatomic world — mostly because the implications of the power of our thoughts to create our reality bumps uncomfortably up against the realm of belief, faith, and religion. Remember that many of these scientists in the 1920s also had faith in their own religious worldview. They were taught to keep faith and science firmly separated. It is all just too weird. It is weird to think of the consequences of every thought and decision you make immediately affecting the basis of all matter. How would one incorporate this information into daily life?

Nope. A decision *was* made. The spooky results of experiments in the subatomic world was a separate field of science and not *at all* connected to the outcome of events in the larger world. This is the world view that has held sway in the scientific world for over **90** years.

Think of it — 90 years of the scientific world suppressing the knowledge that thoughts affect matter.

And the most damaging thing is *not* that they suppressed it from the general public, but they suppressed it from themselves! They ignored one of the most fundamental discoveries in science! They clung to the outdated and absurdly false notion that matter is solid and thoughts are not important. The truth **is** matter is **ephemeral**, intangible, and based on particles that are more like an **idea** than a solid object, and thoughts are the drivers of physical outcomes in the world. Thoughts really do create our reality.

The Buddha said in about 250 BC, "With our thoughts, we create the world." That is the truth. The science behind this statement has been known for 90 years. It is the truth that many teachers of Law of Attraction throughout the ages have taught. Our thoughts are powerful. Our thoughts change matter, our bodies, our experiences. Setting a positive intention is **important**.

If you want your life to change, if you want true and deep happiness, you must first set your clear intention, belief, and focus on that positive outcome.

Setting an Intention

This whole 'thoughts-creating-reality' thing might be terribly intimidating. Just for now, keep your intention simple.

Keep it very simple. "I choose to be happy" is a great intention. That alone will work wonders for you.

Just ask yourself, "How would it feel if this statement was true for me?" Just imagining, daydreaming how that would *feel*, will shift your energy, body-mind, and behaviours on a profound and subtle level.

This play-acting and pretending will bring changes into your life almost instantaneously.

The longer the intention is held, the more momentum is gathered and the more and more evidence will surround you that **your** thoughts are important.

An intention held a short time will create a small effect; an intention held steadily will gather more energy around it, and it will create a large effect. **You** have the power to direct your thoughts wherever you choose. As you develop a steady focus, you gather more energy to you. It is the magnitude of that energy which begins to create change in your life.

Just as when you're driving your car, you have to look where you're going to get there safely. You must focus on the road, not on the ditch. So too must you direct your focus toward your intention to get the results you are seeking.

When you're driving, you have to keep your eyes moving and take in all the information you need. You have to observe the conditions, the road, the other drivers, and pedestrians. You adjust your speed and direction, based on the new information, based on the quick scanning of the moment you're in. But always, *always*, you return your gaze to the direction you're wanting to go. If you make a wrong turn, you go around the block. There is always a way to get there. There is always a way to travel to where you want to be. Focus on the road, not the ditch.

With setting and holding intentions, it is no different. You only want to look at the problem as long as it takes to understand it. From there, you begin moving your thoughts and feelings toward the outcome you desire.

Often, I hear, "I want to be free of this pain." This is not an intention. Yet.

If the word 'pain' is part of the picture in your head, that is all you will continue to get. You need to shift toward what is wanted — ease, freedom of movement, strength, balance, flexibility. These are positive words and bring to mind concrete visuals of activities that can happen when pain is not limiting your life experience.

You can also ask yourself, "How would I live my life differently? How would I feel? What would I be able to do if I was free of my problem? What choices would be different in my life?"

These questions are important to ponder when you're setting a solid, positive intention.

At their core, all intentions and affirmations could be simplified to one pure image of being happy, whole, healthy, and complete. Imagine creating and starring in your own mini-movie entitled "All is Well". Picture yourself laughing, running through a field of daisies, or cuddling puppies and kittens. It is remarkably simple, but highly effective.

Affirmations are Intentions

I strongly recommend the practise of affirmations. Affirmations are an easy way to train the mind to use positive language and for setting a positive intention for any task. Affirmations are simple statements about how you ideally want to feel and think.

When you start using affirmations, you may feel incredibly weird and awkward. Like an SNL skit come to life! But trust me when I say that they work anyway! Practising affirmations may *feel* unsettling at first, but that is just the ego trying to prevent change.

What I have noticed in my work is that if it feels too weird or uncomfortable, people just don't do it. The most transformative practices in the world are completely useless if they are never done.

That is why I created the Affirmation Ladder[*] process. Instead of one giant leap to a positive thought, you can take it in little steps. The Affirmation Ladder process will help you if

---

[*] You can start using the Affirmation Ladders right away. Just go to the appendix at the back of this book and dive in! You can also download your own digital copy from genevarobins.com/affirmationladders.

you have had trouble with using affirmations in the past. It eases you into all this positive thinking crap, bit by bit.

I mean, let's not get crazy!

Positive thinking is downright RADICAL. Especially when your inner critic, the ego, has been in charge for a while.

The Affirmation Ladders for the Reiki Ideals will help you to get past that resistance by offering a thought that is closer to the truth: "This sucks!" And then nudges you a little bit towards the positive: "This sucks, but it will get better, one day, and I'm still a good person."

When you use the Affirmation Ladders, you can nudge the inner critic and ego right out of the way, one tiny step at a time.

Change and the Ego

The ego part of ourselves is mindlessly dedicated to protecting us from further hurts, so it resists any attempt to dislodge worry, fear, or anger. It may seem odd — that we cling to old, unproductive thoughts and behaviours, even though we feel miserable — but it is just our misguided way of trying to keep ourselves safe.

From the standpoint of the ego, if you don't change, you won't get hurt. But you also won't grow, feel joy, or the thrill of accomplishment.

Staying stuck and refusing to change is worse than death. Death, at least, is transformative.

Stagnation is the only thing to be avoided, and it is just what our ego and negative inner critics will encourage us to do.

Life is meant to be experienced, and life's only constant is change.

Making an intention is an act of change. Even if nothing appears different in the outer world, even if we have the exact same problems today as we did yesterday, holding an intention shifts your attitude, your expectations, and eventually, your whole life.

Change is valuable.

Instead of being adrift on a sea of change, setting an intention gives us back our power. Even though change can make us feel vulnerable, moving forward feels better than staying stuck.

It is okay to be stuck!

Getting stuck is juicy!

Just be kind, acknowledge the stuckness for what it is, the ego's attempt to thwart change, and decide to change anyway. Change isn't always comfortable, but it is always necessary.

Divine Love is Available to Everyone — This means you!

A big part of setting an intention is just getting the ego out of the way of all the energy called into our lives, when we hold a positive thought. Most of the time, the only barrier to greater wealth, health, or happiness is our own limiting thoughts and beliefs. We alone are the barrier.

There is a tremendous amount of energy, resources, and abundance available for you. Every time you focus on something you might want, you generate that powerful flow toward you. However, the belief you are not deserving is the primary block to this great energy.

Belief in worthiness or unworthiness is a flawed thought. It is a thought that is directly contrary to the universe's attitude towards you.

Believing you're allowed only a portion of the Universe's love or that you must do or behave in a particular way to earn your rewards is flawed. You are inherently worthy of this great love, only because you exist.

Your existence on this planet is a direct demonstration of Divine Love. You chose to come to this planet to experience the diversity of life and create in a way that is only possible when you are here. God, or Divine Love, responded to your wish to incarnate and delivered you to this amazing place, full of contrast and diversity.

That you're here now, reading these words, is evidence that you are loved.

That is really the true objective of prayer and meditation, to feel God's unlimited, unending, pure love for you. If it were possible for you to really feel that love, for only a moment, it would completely transform any situation within you that feels stuck.

Furthermore, it *is* possible. It is possible, right *now*, where you're sitting, to experience this deep, ecstatic, transformative love. It is only a thought away.

Worthy of Love

The underlying thought of the universe is one of love. Pure, unending, always refilling, infinite, universal, LOVE. It does not need to be earned. It does not require 'good' behaviour. It does not need offerings or prayers or even thanks. It is just there, ever-present, for everyone, all the time.

This LOVE is not judgmental. It does not discriminate. It does not define or separate or label. It is wordless, unformed, abundant. It is in everything, and we are in it. We do not need to do anything to be worthy, because we are already it! It is like asking a fish if it is worthy of the sea. It just is! And so are we. We are all worthy, each and every one of us, of the LOVE of the Universe. I am. You are. We are. Period.

Meditation is Love

The following mediation is a small sample of all the love the Universe has in store for you. The true and vast love available to you is ever present.

This vast source of energy is the energy that is called upon when we access Reiki, use prayer or meditation, or when we feel truly content and happy. It is infinite and eternal. Its nature is accepting and loving. It is non-judgmental and free to all who call upon it. It is not affected by the status, colour, or denomination of the person asking. In this way, it is beyond religious denominations, and yet, a part of the core of truth within each one. Just as the universe is large enough to hold all of the galaxies with their own unique character, Divine Love is large enough to be available and to belong to everyone, regardless of personal belief.

This Law of Inclusiveness, of commonality, is a deeply woven part of the fabric of Divine Love. All conditions, all viewpoints, and all states of being can coexist. There is no friction between disparate ideas, because each idea exists within its own state of energy.

By entering into meditation, you can dip your toe into this infinite pool of Divine Love. The more you meditate, the closer this experience of being loved and supported will be known to you. And once you experience it in meditation, you will see it reflected in the world around you.

Meditation to Expand Divine Love

Begin now:

This is a reading meditation. As you read these words, you will be drawn towards a place of peace and rejuvenation. It is a place you know well. It is a place where your heart is free and light. It is a place where your shoulders drop down your back, and your hands rest easily, softly holding this book. It is a place where your jaw is soft and pliant and where your neck is loose and free. It is a place where your face and its muscles open, relax, and use their energy to softly smile. Sweetly and softly. Smiling. It is a place where your belly is relaxed and soft, filling and emptying with air. Your belly easily flowing with your slow, gentle, and smooth breath. Breathe softly, breathe gently.

Let the soft wave of your breath take on the quality and depth of ocean waves. Gently lapping on the beach, softly in and out. Smoothly, flowing. Let your legs rest easily, gently breathing softness and comfort into every muscle, every tendon, everywhere, Your whole body, soft, pliant, relaxed, open.

Now, gently focus on the energy within your heart. There is a soft, warmness here. It is a physical sensation right in the centre of your chest. Just behind your breastbone, your sternum. This soft energy has a slight buzz to it, a vibration, it feels the same as sunshine, sunlight, but inside. Inside your chest is the same quality of energy as the sun itself. Feel it now. Allow this energy, the energy of your Divine Spark, be known. Be aware of this soft, warm energy. Breath right into the centre of it. Notice how each breath affects the energy you feel. Each breath brings more light, more warmth, more love into your heart space.

Let your breath gently expand this energy to fill your entire chest, right to your back, your shoulder blades, your shoulders, and up the back of your neck. Let the light fill your throat, travelling upwards, filling your mouth and tongue, filling your nose and nasal cavities and sinuses. Let the energy fill your cheekbones and the base of your skull. Let the energy flow and fill the muscles behind your ears and right into the inner ear itself. Let the energy flow up to the top of your skull. Resting easily on the top of your head. Now, let the energy flow into your crown and into your brain. Let the light of your heart illuminate your brain. Let it shine.

You are now ready to step aside a little more and let the intensity of your Divine Spark grow. Let it be brighter. Brighter still.

Allow this Divine energy to flow down and through your body. Filling your mind, your heart, your belly. Let it flow into and expand your back, supporting you. Let it fill your pelvis and hips, stabilizing you. Let it flow down your legs, fill your knees, and flow into each and every toe on your feet. Let this brilliant energy flow down your arms, fill your elbows and wrists, and settle gently and easily into your hands.

Take a deep breath. And let it out.

Let the infinite love the Universe has for you flow in. Let the love flow in. Be willing to let more light in. Let the Divine Love of your Source love you.

Breathe deeply.

Let more love in. Step out of the way of it.

Surrender old habits and negative thinking to the immense love of Source.

Let love replace the old stuff. Let love fill the space.

Let love fill all the empty places in your heart, in your mind, in your body.

Let it all in. Let it all in NOW.

Now, scan your body. Look for tension. Look for ease. Look for any held muscles, any held breath, any tension in your face or scalp. Any holding your breath or belly.

Take a deep breath NOW. Let your breath relax these spaces now.

Let the light fill in these spaces now.

You are enough.

You are loved.

You are appreciated.

You are honoured.

You are loved.

You are loved.

You are loved.

Sharing Circle

In my classes, I have my students participate in Sharing Circles, where a talking stick is passed around the circle, giving everyone a chance to share their experience. When the person is holding the talking stick, they are given full attention, respect, and space to share from the heart. This really allows people to connect and support each other through the deep personal work that meditation can activate.

There is something really healing and transformative about having lovely people hold space for you to share your experiences, thoughts, and feelings. I highly recommend sharing your experiences with others, as you journey through this book. Having other people to share with expands and illuminates your experience.

Even if you don't join a study group, write down your experiences as you journey through the material. Writing in a journal is a phenomenal healing practice all on its own. You give yourself space on the page to acknowledge your true feelings and experiences. Your journal becomes both a powerful tool and an invaluable record of the transformative journey you are on.

Take some time now to write down your experiences with the last meditation. Here are some prompts to help you:

So how did that meditation go?

What feelings or thoughts came up for you?

Did you feel resistance or ease in any parts of your body? Either are just fine. Just observe your response with kindness and acceptance.

Look Inward to Make your Life Change

When you hold a particular idea in your mind, you emit an energy field that surrounds you. This energy flows in degree and magnitude to the strength of the idea and the emotional magnitude it has for you. Strong ideas create strong fields. Strong fields draw people and experiences to you that match the character and intensity of that core thought.

This is important to know when you're setting intentions, repeating affirmations, or just generally going about your day — if your mindset is focused on what is **unwanted** in your life, then you will emit an energy that brings those unwanted experiences right to you. You stay stuck in the same problem only because **your** thoughts and feelings bring more energy to it.

If you deliberately shift your thoughts, if only for a moment, toward what you **do** want, or better still, shift your thoughts and energy to a neutral space through meditation, you will make a profound shift in the character of the energy you emit.

Unhelpful people drift out of your experience. Unhelpful thoughts shift to positive thoughts, and situations appear, as if by magic, bringing you exactly what you desire.

People who hold very different ideas will never meet. Ever. Even if they are in the same room, they might as well be on different planets. They will not see each other and they will not interact.

If, on the other hand, you think a lot about how wrong other people's ideas are, then there is a strong overlap in the energy, because you are focused on what you don't want. You have a concordance of energies with people who hold an opposite viewpoint. You draw them right to you, like a magnet, because you are thinking about how much they annoy you.

External focus is a trap. If you are trying to change your life, you can get distracted by thinking you have to change outer situations to feel different on the inside. This external gaze is a distraction, because the outer world is only a mirror. It only shows us what lives **within** us, on the **inside**. If you are serious about changing your life, you must look **inward**.

Clean up your own mind, your own thoughts, your own feelings, and everything else will shift in response to your **internal** changes. No extra effort required. Action may be needed, but usually that is seemingly effortless, straightforward, practical, and the most obvious next step.

The true work, always, is aligning your thoughts with what you truly desire. When you shift your attention to what you truly want, **everything** changes for the better.

Look at the road, not the ditch!

How to Set an Intention

Okay. Setting an intention is clearly a big deal. But how do you go about that exactly?

First things first — intentions are instructions for the universe.

They are like an address in the GPS navigation system; the most sophisticated piece of equipment in the world will do you no good if you don't use it.

So, just like picking an address, choose your destination. JUST the destination. Leave the details of how to get there to the intelligence of the machine. Leave the details to the Universe. Allow the course to alter as you need it to and follow the guidance as you receive it — turn by turn.

Set your intention by making a clear statement of what you WANT. Use positive, constructive, and inspiring wording. You can keep the statement simple, even just one powerful word, like joyfulness. Or you can use descriptive imagery and whole paragraphs. You can be as simple or detailed as you choose; whatever resonates with you the most is the route for you. Some people love-love-love making collages and vision boards; other people just get paper cuts. No need to force it. If a visual image resonates, use that; if a detailed paragraph, written in calligraphy, resonates, use that; if a song on the radio resonates, use that!

Be clear and focused. Keeping the intention easy for you means you will think about it more often, and it will gradually **become** your life.

Consider this scenario. It's the middle of winter, snow is on the ground outside, and it is sub-zero out there. In the night, your furnace quits working, and you wake up to a cold, cold house. Your nose is cold as you poke your head out of the covers and, even though your blankets are thick and heavy, you are shivering. You get out of bed and walk into your kitchen, where your bare foot hits the icy cold tile. Brrr! You are freezing from head to toe.

In this situation, everything in your experience is cold. You are cold; your house is cold; everything you touch is cold. It is useful to acknowledge this is a problem. It is important to know the house is not at the right temperature. But only focusing on the cold is not making you any warmer! It is only **confirming** the outer circumstances, not actually **changing** them.

It is important to focus on the solution — warmth! The intention is warmth. To warm the house and yourself, you may have to relight the pilot light, you may have to call a furnace repair company, you may have to start a fire in the fireplace, or you may have to make a cup of cocoa. These actions are driven by the intention to become warm.

The difference between confirming the cold and affirming the warmth is huge. Holding the intention of warmth, allowing your actions to be focused on moving towards what you want, brings you to the experience of warmth faster and easier than grumbling about the cold. Focusing solely on what you do **not** want keeps you fixated on the **problem** instead of moving toward the **solution**.

From a sheerly practical perspective, you make choices and take action from the basis of actually being warm once again and that alone means you are one step closer to warmth. From an energetic perspective, the decision and visualization of warmth creates a wave of energy that brings it to you even faster.

If you add into your intention that your furnace will be fixed easily, quickly, and affordably, then you are aligned even more with the state of flow that will bring your desire into your experience. The furnace repair people will be friendly, they will give you good advice, and they will arrive on time and be helpful. If you focus on what you want, you are able to see it when it happens. If you focus on what you don't want, you will miss it. You won't even see all the good things happening, because you were looking the other way.

Think about what you REALLY want in life. *Really* want.

What is it?

Write it down now.

When you think about what you want, are you using words that are just describing your current situation? Are you confirming your lack? Are you trying to get rid of pain? Are you focused on the absence of a partner?

Or are you describing your abundance? Are you focused on ease of movement? Dancing and singing in the kitchen with a wonderful person?

The shift in perspective from *confirming* to *affirming* is huge. It is everything. Happiness is a feeling state. It is a generated by a DECISION — to be happy. It could just be that deceptively simple. Choose to feel happy. Choose to see the joyful moments. Focus on the aspects of life that are fulfilling. Make tiny choices every day that bring some light into the dark places. Choose to light up a smile on someone else's face. These things may be small, but they all add up. Together, a life of tiny joyful moments is one happy life. But you only get it if you look for it, if you choose it. Choose to set an intention to experience these joyful moments and create that joyfulness internally first. Then just sit back and watch your life change.

You are Worthy of Your Intention — Be Willing to Receive it!

Once you have set your intention, the work becomes to get out of the way of the energy that flows to you. Just being **willing** to change is enough to get amazing changes started. Be willing to embrace your power. Be willing to think a new thought. Be willing to be supported by the universe. Supported, not just in energy, but also in time, money, friends, lovers, good weather, and good fortune. Get out of the way of it.

Be willing to recognize the help when it is offered. Be willing to receive. Accept your good and say thank you. Believe you are worthy of this abundance of blessings and so much more goodness in your life. Believe the universe is unlimited and is able to give you **more** than what you're able to ask for. The only difference between 'having' and 'having not' is a simple belief.

So believe! Believe this to be true, for it is. Believe this. Believe in yourself. Love yourself. Have faith in yourself. Know you're worthy of this, right now, for no reason. It does not have to be earned. It just is. It is yours. Say yes! Make room for 'YES!'

CHAPTER THREE:

Get out of the Way!

Ever since happiness heard your name, it has been running through the streets trying to find you.

~ Hafiz

Divine Support is Available and You've got it Pontiac!

The very first thing I teach in Reiki is, if you want the energy to flow freely and purely, you need to get out of the way. There is no push or pull in Reiki. The energy is there. It is universal, infinite, and unlimited. It will flow in quantity and quality in response to the intention set by the person receiving the treatment. It is accurate and precise, and it is tremendously powerful. It is a vast intelligent resource, and it only needs an intention and a willingness to let it flow to work and create amazing results.

Getting out of the way of the vast resources of the Universe is a skill **everyone** needs. It is not limited to the lucky few who have been attuned to Reiki. It flows for everyone, all of the time. It is the force behind the Law of Attraction. It is the Divine Intelligence that supplies all the energies we require to create the life we want. It is the pulse of the Universe, the throb of life that underlies all matter. It flows as easily to you as it does to me. It has no judgment and does not require "good" behaviour to be earned. It is love. Love in its purest and highest form. It is the love that soothes all injury, heals all wounds, and nurtures all who call upon it. It softens the harshness of physical life and uplifts even the darkest of circumstances.

But in order to have this flow of light, love, and energy work for you, you must allow it into your experience. Divine Intelligence works on the Law of Free Will, so it can never assert itself into your experience, without your direct permission and willingness.

You must ask, every single time. If you're reading this book, chances are, this is not new information to you. You already know or have had glimmers of the transcendence and power that can happen when you "Let go and Let God." But, perhaps, you forget to ask sometimes. That is okay if you do. It takes practise, trust, and a deep sense of worthiness to consciously call upon your Divine Resources on a regular and consistent basis.

I know this because it happens to me, as well, usually when I get caught up in the busyness of life. I forget to pause and ask for help. Thankfully, though, those days are fewer and fewer now. I use Reiki to help me be centred in my own knowing. I fill myself up with energy before I help others. I pause in the midst of my day and check into my internal compass, my navigator that tells me if I am moving toward my goals or away from them. But always, I must stop and ask. The Universe loves me enough to not interfere in the lessons I came to this life to learn. So, in its infinite wisdom, it allows you and me to choose our own adventure. But the power is always ours to choose differently.

Take Full Responsibility —
Take on Your Full Power

The true source of all your problems is **you**, standing in your own way.

Oops! Sorry! I seem to have dropped my mike! :)

Take your power back. It is not your boss, your parents, your spouse, your children, your pets, your ex, your neighbours, your acquaintances, or co-workers that are the problem. **You** are the common denominator in your **own** life.

That may seem harsh, especially if you're in the middle of dark times in your life, but I assure you; acknowledging your power to affect every single aspect of your outer world, and taking full responsibility for your experience is the most **empowering** thing you can do and the fastest way out of your problems.

Once you acknowledge, even in a small way, your thoughts, emotions, and energy can powerfully shape your experience, then you will see real change in your life. It goes beyond getting green lights and parking places. You get in the groove, in the flow of life, and all of creation gets out of the way for you.

When you get out of the way, all other obstacles disappear as though vaporized. This is a powerful result of the Law of Attraction working on you. Getting your own limiting beliefs and emotions out of the way, internally, causes a ripple effect in your outer life. The Universe instantly responds to the decrease in resistance within you by providing a decrease in the resistance in your outer world.

And, it goes the other way too! If you look around your world, you will see any number of areas in your life offering resistance to you. You could be confronted with bad traffic, arguments with your children, distance from your spouse, an unsatisfying job, lack of finances, or any other outer situation that seems to be limiting your happiness. I encourage you to stop playing victim. Stop placing blame and fault and take full responsibility for every aspect of your life.

Say What!?! — Yes. It's All Up to You.

Ugh! Seems like a lot doesn't it? You may want to breathe a little bit here. You might be tempted to swing into emotions of overwhelm, anger, vulnerability, self-reproach, loathing, and just generally being down on yourself.

That is okay! That is normal. That is a normal reaction, especially if this is a new concept for you. That is a normal reaction if this if something you have known for a long time, but keep slipping back into the victim role. But, trust me; it won't take long to get results, no matter how small at first, that will show you the power you have when you bring back your source of true power in your life, your ability to master your thoughts, emotions, and energy.

Let's just say you can suspend disbelief long enough to agree, temporarily of course, that the inner world mirrors the outer world and vice versa. If that is the case, then you have two powerful resources at your disposal — you can shift your inner landscape to include more thoughts of wanted things and situations, *and* you can use your outer world as an indicator of how well you're doing in your ability to master your inner dialogue. In both cases, you're not taking any action; you're not *doing* anything. You're not quitting your job, leaving your spouse, or running away. You're simply *observing* your connection between your inner world and your outer world.

A dialogue goes back and forth between the inner and outer worlds. The dialogue is composed of energy, emotion, and vibration, just the non-physical, non-matter stuff the Universe can hear. When you set an intention, the emotion you feel begins to shift you. If you don't resist that shift in vibration, you create a wave of energy that shifts actual matter. Your experience can change overnight. Just allowing the changes to happen can be the biggest task.

You Matter to Matter

Suppose, for a moment, we could have access to a vast 3D imaging computer, like the one in the movie Iron Man 2, where Robert Downey Jr., as Tony Stark, can sweep away with the flick of a finger, all of the extraneous information and just hone in on the most relevant details of the problem he was trying to solve. Now consider that this super-duper computer is able to represent the city or town where you live in remarkable detail, right down to the flowers in the flower beds and leaves on the trees. You can zoom out to any level. The whole world is accurately displayed and is at your fingertips. With a flick of a finger, we can swipe away the buildings, trees, grass, and flowers; we can remove the other people, and we can even get ourselves out of the picture. Now we can go further; we can swipe away the ground and the sky, and our accomplishments and possessions, labels, attributes, and even our bodies.

Now... what is left?

Remember, this is an accurate representation of the Universe. It is not nothing. It is definitely **something**. What is it? Can you perceive the energy here? Can you sense the awareness sensing you sense it? What is here? What remains when all traces of matter have been swept away?

Energy, yes. Energy is here, but that is a thin word for the resonance that is felt. It is a resonance that feels like a deep, low sound that hums in the centre of your teeth and below your sternum. Deep in the bones. That presence, that awareness, that listening to the listener, that is where it can be felt. Even more, that deep consciousness in the Universe can be known, not just by you and me, but by everyone. It does not discriminate. It does not differentiate. It does not define or label. It ignores status, possessions, and all other indications of past actions. It does, powerfully and strongly, respond and know emotions and energy that hit the same frequency.

Think of a low sound that vibrates a glass on a coffee table. The glass rattles only when the sound is produced long enough, low enough, and loud enough. Your emotional and energy states are the same. The Universe 'hears' you best when you're consistent in your positive intention, when you repeat it frequently and with enough intensity. This beautiful mechanism prevents our surface thoughts from disrupting our daily lives. We can still dream and day-dream and ponder. We can still watch movies and read books that deal with scenarios we would not want to personally experience. The deepness of the signal to the Universe must be like that low, deep hum left in the space when all other "things" were removed. That conscious, definite, perceptible hum, the vibration of the Universe. Your deeply held convictions, longings, and desires are all vibrating at deep tones.

Deep in your bones...What do you feel? What is true for you? Do you want that to continue to be true for you? You can change it. You can alter the signal you're sending to the Universe. You can change your deeply held beliefs about what is possible for you, and you can begin to see tremendous and practical changes in your outer life.

In this whole scenario, you're at centre stage. You are the main player, and the Universe responds uniquely to you and only you, with just what you're wanting. At the same precise moment, the universe is responding to the countless numbers of conscious beings, each making their own choices and decisions and sending their own, low, deep tones that the Universe can also hear. Everyone has this power to shape their own lives. Not all of them know it. Many run on the decisions they have been told to make and think the thoughts they have been told to think. As they do, they get highly predictable lives.

I have never been one to fit in. Even when I really wanted to, there was always some odd corner of my true self, sticking outside of the bounds. And I suspect, if you're reading this, you're an independent, wise one yourself. I cannot teach you to fit in and be 'normal', but I can teach you to be yourself. You can discover what really makes your heart sing. You can become all you have wanted to be. You can reach for your unlimited stars, full of possibilities and adventure. It is all here for you. Right now, waiting, for a clear steady signal that you really want it.

Practice

Just for Today — Become Aware

For the next day, notice your internal dialogue.

Notice when your dialogue supports your positive intention for change. Notice when your inner dialogue gets in the way of your intention. Pay attention to the feeling in your body when you encounter a thought of support or a thought of resistance, getting in the way.

How does each type of thought feel? What happens to your energy levels? What happens to your urges to indulge in addictive or numbing behaviours?

Right now, you're just noticing. Just observe these thoughts as you would strangers on a busy sidewalk. Each one comes and goes, and you have particular reactions to them. Just notice the reaction in your body; notice your habitual impulses. At this stage, it is enough to just notice them.

It is like walking down a busy street, staring at your phone, and then suddenly looking up. You see everything around you, but in a new way. Before, you were unaware, but now you are bringing awareness, light, to the new part of your inner landscape. Trust that in the course of reading this book, you will learn the tools to shift the inner dialogue to supportive and uplifting words. Over time, as you work through the material, you will feel the full body resonance of those new positive thoughts. And you will perceive how your thoughts and emotions communicate with the deep pulse of the Universe.

Be easy with yourself. Every time you notice a negative, getting in the way thought, you have an opportunity to shift towards the positive. Becoming *aware* of repetitive and unhelpful thoughts and feelings is the first step in getting out of the way.

Just for today... become aware.

Jump in the Stinky Pond

How did that practice go? Did you notice all the "should's" your mind cooked up to keep you small? How about numbing and addictive behaviours? It is totally normal to have an increase in these unhelpful thoughts and behaviours when you're attempting a change. It is like stirring up the bottom of a stagnant pond. Debris rises to the surface, it is unsightly, and it probably stinks.

That stink is just resistance. Resistance is actually a really good thing! Uncomfortable, but good.

At this point, you may think, "Why bother? Why change at all if the process is so uncomfortable, so unpleasant? Isn't all this love and light crap supposed to make me feel better?"

If that sounds like you, that is totally alright!

While staying stuck, staying stagnant, may seem comfortable on the surface because it is known and familiar. It is actually deeply uncomfortable.

It is even worse than that!

It is soul crushing. It is a suffocating way of existence and not at all why you incarnated here on this amazing planet in the first place.

You would not have encountered this book or even be reading this sentence if you were interested in leading a stuck and stagnant life.

In order to return to the flow of life, to reconnect to the vast and unlimited energy the Universe has for you, you must hop in the pond, pull up the weeds choking the life out of you, and get the limiting behaviours and thoughts out of your way.

This uncomfortable part of the process does not last forever and need not take a lot of time. Very soon, you will begin to feel better and vibrant life will return to your inner landscape.

Self Care & Love

The care and feeding of you! Do you have instructions? Have you written down all the little things that nourish you and make you feel whole?

Every single one of us needs love to survive. It is hard wired into our nervous systems. Babies who are not cuddled, even though they are well cared for in every other way, they just give up and die. Failure to thrive.

When we become adults our needs are less intense than when we were babies, but we still need love and care. The biggest thing that changes is that, now, we can meet all of those needs ourselves. We don't have to wait.

Since the outer world is merely a mirror for the inner world, we don't have to wait for another person to love us in order to feel love. In fact, if we do not love ourselves first, no amount of external love will fill us up.

You can start today. You can show yourself the love and appreciation you want from others. Be kind to yourself. Have some me-time. Do things you enjoy and light you up on the inside.

Putting self care and love into practice in your life will be a game changer. Start now.

Signs of Spring

Now for a little process to bring some sweetness into your journey. I call this one **Signs of Spring**.

The winters of our lives can be hard. They can be lonely. They are bare and cold periods, when nothing seems right and nothing seems to be going your way. Nothing works and everything seems frozen with no clear path ahead. You can sometimes lose faith that summer will ever come. But just as with the seasons, summer always arrives. Always. Every year. Guaranteed.

It is the same for you. Hard times are replaced by easy times. Or at least, easier times. It is the cyclical nature of life. We encounter a challenge, we learn, we grow, and we return to happiness, if even for a moment. The point of this book is to extend those times of ease and happiness and to increase their volume. The point of this exercise is to begin looking for tiny signs the winter is leaving and that joy, peace, love, and abundance are here and getting bigger every day.

Signs of Spring are little indications that things are shifting in your life. It is looking for the first signs of warmth, of spring, of tiny seeds germinating in the soil and pushing their way up through the ground. It is the buds on the trees getting fatter and the birds returning. It is a slightly longer day and a beam of sunlight through dark clouds. It is melting and a hush in the air in the pause between dusk and dawn. It is the soft mossy scents of earth returning to its fullness, a stretch, long and delicious and slow after a long slumber. It is waking and rising and returning to what is soft and good and new. It is a softness in the heart. It is a smile from a stranger. It is having the door held for you. It is a small, tiny gesture that the Universe has heard you and summer is on its way.

Get a nice little journal or notepad you can keep near you throughout your day. Keep it with you, in your pocket, in your purse, in your car, by your bedside table, wherever you will remember it and have it close. *At least once a day*, write down your Signs of Spring.

Write down a list every day of these small ways things are getting better. Write down all your successes. Write down the tiniest detail as a symbol your request to the Universe has been heard. If you're wanting more abundance, it could be finding a penny on the street, or a friend buying your coffee, or even an improved feeling in your heart. If you're looking for romance, it could be a smile from a passerby, it could be feeling good about yourself, it could be an increase in synchronicity, or reconnecting with old friends. If you're wanting a better job or more fulfilling work, it could be an unexpected phone call from a co-worker, or someone asking you what your dream job is, or a colleague being friendly. If you're wanting more happiness or improved mood, it could be a chuckle you had when talking to a friend, or waking up to bird song, or watching a beautiful sunset, or playing with your pets, children, or other lighthearted beings.

Write down all the ways, tiny and grand, the changes you desire are occurring. Nurture these tiny sprouts by noticing them and appreciating them when they happen. When you do this, you not only feel better about where you are right now, but you also shift, through Law of Attraction, the vibration you're sending to the Universe. You then begin to powerfully attract more of what is wanted in your life and less of the unwanted.

A tiny bit of appreciation goes a very long way toward improving your mood and creating a new life. Throughout the rest of this book, you will see Signs of Spring Sections pop up, and you will get a prompt to write down your little blessings.

Ooh! Look! Here is one now! :)

Signs of Spring — Start Right Now!

Today your life begins. Begins again. Restart. New chances. New changes.

Today is the day your life changes. Write down this date. Write down why you're grateful that, on this very day, as you read this, your life changed for the better, and you never looked back.

Today is the day.

The Changes Have Already Begun

These prompts to write down your Signs of Spring are little guideposts on your journey through your personal transformation. You will be a different person at the end of this book than the beginning. Signs of Spring will help you keep perspective on where you have been and how far you have come. There are always Signs of Spring for those who look for them. Even in the dead of winter, there is potential and possibility. There is always hope, even if it is tiny at first.

People on a journey always have new ground to cover, new projects to create, and old problems to solve. There is a forward momentum, a progression, to it all. So even if you have new areas of growth and expansion in your life, you will come to see you are moving toward the life you want to live. And one day, very soon, you will wake up and find you are living it.

Intuition

Everyone is intuitive. Everyone. Even you! For reals!

While you build and develop your intuitive muscles throughout the exercises in this book, know that you're already deeply intuitive. Intuition is an innate sense. It extends your sensory experience and combines the millions of bits of information that your body-mind receives every second into an understandable impulse that can guide and protect you.

Intuition is something we are born with. Each one of us is intuitive in our own way. The key is to grow and develop these natural gifts, so you can use it in your life. The more you use your intuition, the clearer it gets, so don't worry if you feel cloudy right now. In time, your intuition will be a strong guide as you make choices and decisions in your life.

Follow Your Own Compass

Your intuition is your compass. It points you toward where you need to go. No matter where you are, it will direct you toward your intention if you are wise enough to listen to it.

Your intuition is wise. It will pick the best path to your destination. Your intuition understands the complexities of your whole life. It is inherently holistic. It sees you and where you are now. It sees the path ahead that will best meet your needs in the moment, while also moving you steadily toward your goals, dreams, and desires.

The *best* path is not always the shortest one. Think of hiking up a mountain. The mountain is very steep, very tall. Some parts of the mountain have loose and falling rock; some parts are thick forests with tall trees and uneven ground. You need to follow your own wise guidance to get to the top safely.

Switchbacks are often the easiest and most accessible way of hiking to the top of the mountain. They are not the most direct route, nor the quickest. They wind and turn and meander. Most of the time you're travelling on a switchback, you're moving crosswise to the top of the mountain, only then to turn briefly toward the top and then continue on in the other direction. And so it goes; slowly and steadily you make it to the top.

Of course there are a multitude of ways to reach the top of a mountain. You could climb if you had the inclination, know-how, and adventurous spirit. You could take a helicopter if you had the resources. You could take a gondola, a car, or you could even shoot yourself out of a cannon!

What is the best route for you? Is that path always the best way? In every area of your life?

The switchback route is often the most common one for the big changes in our lives. Regardless of the method, there are times when you might feel like you're pointed in the wrong direction. You might have your logical mind try to tell you to stop, that you're going the wrong way, but that would be incorrect. Your intuition is your guide — your truest and best way of telling if you're moving closer to your dreams or further away from them.

Activate your Hidden Wisdom

Your intuition can communicate to you in many ways. One of the most important is through the sensations in your body. Your whole body is like an antenna for your spirit. Messages can be received from the non-physical, energetic part of you and 'heard' directly within your body.

Take a moment, now, and take a deep breath. Right down to your belly. Breathe deeply again, this time letting go of the tension in your jaw, your shoulders, your hips, and legs. Breathe easily.

Breathing consciously in this way, you can bring awareness to the overall level of tension in your body. When you breathe, scan your body; where has the tension accumulated? Consciously relax the parts of your body that are tense. Observe the connection between the tension in your body and your thoughts.

You can relax the body by relaxing the mind. You can relax the mind by relaxing the body.

Try this now.

Notice the thoughts you're having in this moment. There is no good or bad to it. No judgment. It just is.

Ask yourself: 'If this thought was connected to a place in the body, where would it be?' Locate the part of the body connected to your current thought. Is that part of your body open or closed? Is it tense, hot, cold, tingling, or normal? Take a deep breath and let the breath relax that area in the body. Almost immediately, the thought shifts as well.

There is a direct connection between your thoughts and emotions, and your body. Just by becoming aware of the tension levels in your body and how your body responds to different thoughts and situations is a first step in turning up the volume on your intuition. Your body is dynamic and responsive to the moment by moment changes in your internal and external environment. The wisdom in your body is clear and easy to interpret with just a bit of practice.

Your Body-mind is a Powerful Intuitive Tool

Often, we distance ourselves from our bodies. Our thoughts and emotions truck along, and our bodies are just carried along for the ride. But when we pause and observe our bodies, we can instantly detect what is true for us and the best path to take. We begin to *feel* again.

When you're following your true path through life, your whole body is relaxed. You move easily; there is no hint of procrastination or resistance. You just flow. You are *in* the flow and nothing can stop you. There is great ease in every part of your body. It just feels right.

Conversely, when you're going against your deep knowing, you feel resistance and anxiety. You get knots in your stomach, and you move slowly. You get block after block, and it feels like the whole universe is against you (it is not). It feels like swimming upstream, you are exhausted, efforting, and going nowhere.

Your whole body tells you if you are off course. Your whole body tells you when you are moving in the right direction. In any given moment, you might have any number of options available to you. Your intuitive body-mind will always indicate which direction is better for you. Just breathe deeply; consciously connect to your body-mind dynamic and *feel* how each option affects the tension in your body.

Intuition, while partly innate, is also a skill; it is a muscle. It takes time to build and strengthen it so it is clear and reliable. At first, as you are building your intuitive muscle, limit your intuitively-based choices to small things. Don't jump right into big life decisions here. Practice first with the small choices.

Take some time to learn how your body responds in certain situations. Notice how it feels in your body when you say yes when you really mean no. Notice how you feel within your body after watching certain TV shows or after talking to certain people. Right now, you are just bringing awareness to the relationship between your physical tension and your life experience.

As you progress through the book, you will access your intuitive powers in deeper and deeper ways. Your intuition will begin to guide you clearly through every situation you may face. You will find that, once you develop this relationship with how your body instinctively responds to your right path, you will also, gradually, in the perfect time, develop a deeper connection with your spiritual guides, angels, totem spirits, and the ascended masters. You will develop the ability to communicate directly to these spiritual resources in a reliable and clear way. You will be able to have clear and immediate access to all this and more. And it all starts with developing your connection with your body.

Just for Today — Listen to Your Body

Over the course of the day, listen to the wisdom within your body. Just listen for now. Note how you feel in different situations. Observe how you feel with different people. What brings your body ease? What makes your body tense up? How does your breathing change? Just observe.

Just for today... listen to the deep intuitive wisdom within your body.

Your Intuition Is Already Getting Stronger!

Your intuition can signal many things to you. It can let you know which direction to take in life. It can also tell you when you are in your own way and the best method to get out of the way of all you desire.

After listening to your body for a day, you probably noticed times when you were particularly tense and times when you were relatively relaxed. There is no right or wrong in it. Maybe you were a bundle of nerves constantly, and you did not ever perceive a time when you relaxed. That is okay too.

The simple act of observing is enough to start tapping into your inner wisdom.

Meditation

Meditation is one of the most effective ways of getting out of the way and into the flow. With only a few minutes a day, you can radically transform your life and expand your intuition.

Keep your meditation practice simple and short, at least, at first. It is more important *that* you meditate daily than the actual length of time you sit. Just set a timer, close your eyes, and breathe. That is it.

Getting out of the Way Feels Good

Your inner wisdom knows the path that is right for you. When you are following your inner guidance system, you feel relaxed, at peace, just right. This is the same feeling you get when you are out of the way. When you are out of the way of the energy available to you, you feel good. When you are in the way, you feel blocked, tense, anxious, irritable, and easily angered.

When you are in your **own** way, you react strongly to any hint of obstacles that might be in your path. You get angry at delays; you resort to blaming and victim thinking. Even tiny disruptions become big problems when **you** are blocking yourself. When you are **out** of the way and in the flow of life, these same tiny obstacles are tackled in stride. Nothing can slow you down. Any obstacle is approached as an opportunity for growth, a challenge to be overcome. When you are out of the way, you can easily solve even large problems, because you are no longer resisting the immense support available to you in terms of ideas and energy, and in people, resources, and great timing. You can't miss. Everything flows.

Sounds great, right?! So now, the challenge is to practice the feeling of getting out of the way when it is easy, so you can get out of the way when it is hard.

The easiest and most reliable method for practicing getting out of the way is through meditation. When you meditate, you develop the skill for calming and focusing the mind. You learn to direct your thoughts, to put your attention on whatever you choose for as long as you choose.

Meditation is mind training. To me, it feels like hitting the reset button on my brain. I get a chance to observe the order or lack of order in my thoughts and deliberately focus on helpful thoughts.

Letting Go Meditation

The easiest and most effective meditation practice that I use daily is this Letting Go Meditation. The rules are very simple. Any thought that causes tension in the body is released. You can visualize handing it over to the Divine, your spirit guide, Master Usui, Jesus, the angels, or any other supportive figure with your best interests at heart. If any tension pops up in your body, you consciously relax that part of your body. You can use your breath to breathe away or through any troublesome thoughts or emotions.

We just set aside some time where we declare, for the next 5 minutes, "I am here to relax. Anything else will have to wait."

During the meditation, you can set aside your thoughts as easily as taking off a heavy backpack. You just put it down and move it off to the side. You can always pick up any thoughts you set aside later. Sometimes knowing you can come back to your worries makes it easier to set them aside. We know that we can always carry on being concerned about our problems on the other side of the meditation.

Sometimes, we carry quite a bit of worry and tension in our body-minds just as a way of not letting things fall through the cracks. Worrying can feel like you are **doing** something about a problem you do not know how to solve or you have no control over. In reality, worrying is just fear thoughts chasing themselves around in your head. Worry doesn't actually **do** anything at all.

Even though worry is one of the **least** effective ways of solving problems, it can feel like being lazy or being inattentive or uncaring if we stop worrying or let go of our tension. Just like being busy, worry and stress can be a badge of honour. Our tension shows the world just how 'good' we are and just how much we care. But this is all false. Worry, tension, and stress inhibit your ability to bring the best of yourself to the world.

Hanging on to worry is the ego-self at work. The ego is the part of us that is invested in staying stuck. The ego is often in charge of habitual reactions and patterns and is naturally resistant to the change that meditation can bring. THIS is the real reason people don't like meditation. It has nothing to do with being bored or not being able to sit still. People don't like meditation because it creates change and the ego will kick up a mighty fuss if you start changing things, even if it is change for the better.

The exact same thing happens with new exercise regimes and changes to a more healthful diet. The part of us that fears change throws up resistance and tries to find ways to avoid the very thing that would help you the most.

If you make a deal with your ego-self that you are only putting aside your tension for 5 minutes, and you can come right back to it as soon as you are done, then you often are able to go much deeper in the meditation. You basically trick the fearful part of you, and you are then able to have much better experiences in meditation. You reach a joyful and expanded state more quickly and reliably if you are aware of your own resistance patterns, than if you had not been conscious of your ego-self's attempts to thwart your meditative practice.

Sometimes you need to dodge your ego a bit and trick it with a distraction so you can get down to the business of meditation.

For the next 5 minutes — Let Go

So here it is — for the next 5 minutes (set a timer), you will consciously relax your physical body. You will deliberately give any worries, concerns, or tension over to your guides and angels or any other Divine being that has your back, and you will remember to breathe.

This is the process of getting out of the way. It is the essence of letting go. Start this practise right now.

I mean, literally, right now.

If you are in a public place, where it might be weird to close your eyes for 5 minutes, then go to the bathroom. I get a lot of great meditation done on a bathroom break. No one interrupts you as long as you keep it to under 5! Otherwise, set your timer on your phone or watch and get going!

Go on! I'll meditate while I am waiting for you to finish meditating.

—

Well done! You did it! You just took a first and most important step toward happiness.

When you develop a meditative practice, your body-mind learns to trust you. You get in the habit of letting stuff go during meditation, so it gets easier and easier. You practice meditation when it is easy, when it is quiet, when you don't have any demands on your time, at the end of the day, before bed, or in the morning before you start your day. You close your eyes to help you filter out distractions, you choose silence or pleasant music to help you focus your hearing. It is easiest to meditate when life is going well. On easy days, meditation is usually easy too. You build your practice slowly, day by day, so when you have a bad day, meditation can help soothe the harshness.

Meditation is a universal balm for the tired, anxious, and angry soul. It calms everything down and gives you perspective. Even on days when your meditation feels more like a mental wrestling match than a blissful experience, you still receive tremendous benefit from meditating. I would say, from personal experience, the times when it is the hardest to meditate are the times when you need it the most. Those are also the times when you get the most benefit, even if it doesn't seem that way. It is really important to meditate anyway. Aim to have some terrible meditations this week. Really awful, chattering mind, can hardly sit still, meditations.

Aim to fail. Do it badly. But just do it. Just sit for 5 minutes every day and be still. Let go of the junk between your ears once a day. Let your body rest. Let your muscles get long and elastic. Untie those knots.

Just keep returning, again and again, and you will see a shift in your ability to let go of tension and anxiety in the other 1,435 minutes of the day! It is not how long you spend in meditation that will transform you. It is how often you return. Come back to it again and again. Even when you don't want to. Especially then! Your whole life will change.

From this point on in the book, you will see **Stop and Give me 5** sections pop up every now and then. These sections are a prompt to do a 5-minute meditation, right then and there!

Oh! Hey! Look! Here comes one now!

Stop and Give me 5!

Be brave. Don't cheat.

Set your timer for 5 minutes. You can do it.

Meditating now, right now, will singlehandedly transform your meditative practice, your inner landscape, and your outer world.

Just be still and breathe.

Sharing Circle

Spend a few minutes now writing in your journal.

How did the meditation shift your experience?

Do you see things differently?

How stressed do you feel, compared to before the meditation?

Affirmations are Intentions

As you develop your awareness of your inner and outer world, you may begin to notice changes in your life. These changes can be shaped and guided by your positive intentions and affirmations. Even if you are not seeing a big shift right now, a positive intention can completely change your perspective and literally change your body[*] and your life.

Getting out of the way of the flow of Divine Support can also be accomplished by setting an intention and repeating it as an affirmation. Affirmations are powerful, positive statements that change your brain and body chemistry when you speak them. That shift in your thoughts and biochemistry causes a ripple effect, so every single cell in every single organ in your body becomes aware of the new thought pattern.

Information chemicals, tiny little peptides, carry the intent behind your affirmations right to each cell in your body. Dramatic and lasting healing can happen when you change your thoughts in this way.

Your energy signal to the Universe also shifts. One positive statement can counteract hundreds of negative ones. The Universe is primed to 'hear' your positive words louder than your negative ones. That is why we still have a world and a solar system and sun. A moment's negativity, even several thousand lifetimes of negativity, is not enough to blow it all up and have it all spin into chaos.

Your positive thoughts are on a megaphone as far as the Universe is concerned. That is why you *only* need to repeat an affirmation several hundred times a day to counter the nearly 60,000 thoughts you could have in a day that might be negative or neutral. A small amount of effort creates enormous results, especially when that effort is directed toward something that makes your soul sing with joy.

---

[*] Check out *Molecules of Emotion* by Candace Pert or *The Biology of Belief* by Bruce Lipton for more about information chemicals and the mind-body connection.

Louise Hay is Awesome!

At this point, I absolutely have to pay a humble homage to Louise L. Hay. She has done more for my personal development than any other author I have ever read. And that is saying *a lot*, because I have so many authors and mentors, who have helped me with my own personal healing journey. Louise's book, *You Can Heal Your Life* is, bar none, the best book on the mind-body connection you will ever read. If you do not have a copy, you need to put this book down, right now, and get one. Really! It is that good.

I use *You Can Heal Your Life* as a text book in all of my classes. It has an amazing list in the back with hundreds of health conditions, their mental causes, and the affirmation that antidotes the pattern in both the mind and the body.

But that is not all! Louise shares her story of how she used these techniques, the power of affirmations, to heal herself of cancer. And, she shares a recipe for getting past resistance and healing not only your body, but your work, your relationships, and your finances. Tremendous resource! Go get it!

Phew! Where was I before I got hit by a tsunami of gratitude? Oh yes! Affirmations!

Working with Affirmations

To get the most out of your practice with positive affirmations, you will want to *feel* how each one resonates with you. Sometimes affirmations may sound great and look good on paper, but we do not really *feel* them as real or true for us. We might intellectually know an affirmation might be true for some people, but we have trouble making the leap to *feeling* it for ourselves.

And it really is the *feeling* of an affirmation that makes the biggest difference to our bodies, our minds, and our imprint on the universe. So as you practice the affirmations in each chapter, pause and become aware of the tension or ease within the body.

Explore how it would feel if that affirmation was true for you. You don't even need to feel it now, today. For right now, you just need to **pretend** you are experiencing the affirmation being true for you.

Pretending is the same as being. As far as the Universe is concerned, your imagined experiences and your actual experiences are interchangeable. So you receive tremendous benefit from a few minutes of daydreaming and play-acting than you would from hours of boring recitation of a sentence you neither felt nor believed.

Now, don't get me wrong. Repetition is important here. You are basically choosing to change your repetitive negative thoughts into repetitive positive ones. The more trouble you are having right now with negative thoughts, including any negative thoughts you might have about how this won't work for you, the **more** you need to practice positive affirmations!

Visualise what it would be like if THIS was true for YOU

God, the Divine, the Universe, the Earth herself, loves me and supplies me with all I ask for.

I eagerly ask for what I need and I joyously accept these precious gifts.

I step aside and make room in my life for all the good the Universe has in store for me.

I allow all the Love that is unconditionally mine to flow in NOW!

I am loved, and I am protected, and I am deserving of all this and more.

I say YES, and I say THANK YOU!

Just for Today — Affirm the Change is Real

Read over the above affirmation several times today. Feel it on the inside. Try it on. Pretend. Play-act in front of the mirror. Notice how your body changes when you mull it over.

Assume it is true and let it guide you. Write it out in loopy letters in your journal. Sing it in the shower. Let the words wash over you and feel the resonance within your spirit.

Fling the doors wide open and get ready to receive all the good the Universe can muster. Which is to say, infinite, endless, arriving in the perfect amount and the perfect time. Your life will get as good as you can handle it. Get ready!

CHAPTER FOUR:

Letting Go of Anger

We can never obtain peace in the outer world until we make peace with ourselves.

~ Dalai Lama

The Reiki Ideals are very simple instructions for living a happy life. Really, living a life guided by the Reiki Ideals is an assurance of happiness.

It is interesting that the first key to happiness is letting go of anger. Simple, right? Well, it will be.

Anger is an uncomfortable emotion. In its uncontrolled state, it can be like a raging inferno, blindly destroying all that is precious and dear to us. One fit of rage is enough to obliterate friendships, damage reputations, lose a job, destroy relationships, and hurt the ones you love the most in this world.

It is easy to understand why we naturally, as 'nice' people, shy away from anger, flee angry situations, and avoid angry people, including ourselves!

Anger is suppressed and avoided at all costs. The damage, as we have learned from experience, anger can cause is too painful to experience. The problem is not the anger, though; it is how we deal with anger. Angry thoughts and feelings have a force and momentum behind them. They either go outward in an explosion, or inward in an implosion. Either way, tremendous damage can be done by out of control anger.

But there is a third option with anger; we can let it go. This is completely different from controlling or suppressing anger. And it is not the same as "blowing off steam." With this method, you are spotting anger *before* it arises and choosing a different experience. You let go of anger in an instant when you choose to feel a different emotion.

The Mechanics of Anger

Anger is Addictive

In the modern Reiki Ideals, it is phrased this way. "Just for today, I will not anger." If you know the AA or 12 step program philosophy, this phrasing will sound familiar. Just for today, I will not drink (or use, or compulsively eat or gamble). There is an acknowledgment in addictions counseling that nearly any compulsive behaviour can be curbed or managed if we take a tiny bit of time (a day, an hour, a minute, even a second) and commit to choosing a different behaviour.

There is a direct acknowledgment anger is a compulsive behaviour we indulge in when we lack the inner tools and resources to solve our problems in other ways.

Being angry is a choice. Staying angry is a choice. If anger is a choice, then we have a real opportunity to make a different choice.

There is no accident that problems with anger can be connected to other addictive behaviours. In some ways, it is easy to stop drinking, using, overeating, or gambling, but it is harder to stop uncontrolled anger.

That is because there is a huge, seductive, satisfying, pleasurable pay-off when we get angry. It feels good. It feels powerful. You have control of the room if you are the angriest one in it. Other people shrink away and let you have what you want.

You can control and manipulate other people's behaviour and have them listen to you. Sometimes, the only way you can be sure you are heard is when you fly off the handle, and everyone stops what they are doing and addresses your concerns. Anger is powerful. Anger inspires action. Anger creates change.

BUT — and that is a big but! — but anger never achieves the results you really want. It never gets the perfect solution. It never motivates others for long. It damages relationships beyond repair, and it damages you too. After the euphoria of the angry outburst is over and you survey the wreckage you have caused in your life, you invariably get overcome with feelings of remorse, depression (anger turned inward), sadness, helplessness, and even self-loathing.

The True Purpose of Anger

So anger is not really the best way to deal with problems, but it is not 'bad' either. Anger is just an emotion. And all emotions have their place and their purpose.

The most important thing to know about anger is that it is meant to inspire *action*. When we are threatened or vulnerable, anger calls us to take action. If we are feeling disempowered, depressed, or attacked, anger is not only an appropriate response, it is *healthy*. Anger has its purpose. It can give us the fire we need to change intolerable circumstances.

Anger is inherently empowering when you are in serious trouble and you need to take *action* to survive or escape. Anger is powerful. There are many situations where anger can keep us safe.

Anger is one of our oldest and most primal emotions. It is linked to our flight, fright, or freeze response, the burst of adrenaline we get when we need to protect ourselves. When we are faced with a stressful, life-threatening event, anger towards a predator or competitor could assure our survival; at least, it would have in the early days of humanity. Anger can inspire huge amounts of physical strength and agility. It is frightening. An enraged human can easily scare away bears and lions. Of course, we are all bark with no bite where large predators are concerned, but they don't know that! Angry people survived.

Anger can be an incredibly powerful force for change. Think of how you hold your body when you feel depressed. You shrivel up; you are immobile; you avoid eye contact; you rarely speak. Now, consider your body position when you are angry. Your eyes flash; you look directly at your opponent; you pace and move your arms; you talk loudly and shout; you stand tall and square your shoulders toward your attacker. Which one gets more done? Which way of being creates change? Which one is better? How long can it last?

In this scenario, where you only have depression or anger to choose from, anger is clearly the better choice. Instead of enduring an unacceptable situation, anger gives you the force and momentum to change it. You can take action very easily when you are angry. In this case, anger serves a valuable purpose. When conditions are extreme, anger seems to be the best way out.

Anger was never meant to be a chronic condition. Anger helped us frail humans survive, but it was only useful in the moment of threat. After the initial situation was over, anger and the biochemistry behind it, like adrenaline and cortisol, would dissipate and peace would return to the mind and body.

The biggest problem with anger is that it is blind emotion; you cannot see what you are doing when all you can see is red. The choices you make when you are in the grips of anger are often not the choices you would make if you were sober and thinking rationally. If we leave anger to steer the boat, we will inevitably sink. We go down with the ship. The long-term cost of anger is damage to health, relationships, and careers; it is just too high a price to pay.

On a Hair-trigger: How to Lengthen your Fuse

The emotion of anger is linked to our stress state. We can see this link in our own lives after a bad night's sleep. How patient are you in traffic, with your spouse, or with your kids the next day? If our bodies are filled with adrenaline and cortisol on an ongoing basis, then our minds are primed for anger. We are on a hair-trigger, set to explode at the least thing.

It goes way back to that instinctive part of our brains. Our brains say, "If I am this stressed, then there must be real danger, and I am going to fight my way out."

Not a bad strategy if the actual stressor is something trying to eat you.

Often though, it is usually not an actual life threatening situation, just the daily accumulation of busy, stressful, modern life. We are always on. Never stopping. Always rushing. Bombarded by news and media warning us of impending catastrophe around every corner. Unless we stop.

Unless we stop and take a moment to deliberately rest the mind and the body, the stress builds and builds.

There is an easy way to reset the mind-body.

Meditation.

Yeah, I know. "How can I meditate at a time like this!?!?" Trust me. Even a lousy, busy-mind, angry meditation will dramatically shift your stress state. It just takes five minutes.

Meditation offers us a powerful chance to deliberately lower our stress levels. It gives us some space to breathe. It calms down the whole body-mind and allows creative and constructive solutions to rise to the surface. We insulate ourselves against random and uncontrolled fits of anger. By outsmarting our biology during a few minutes of meditation, we can uncouple the stress equals anger equation, and we can begin making new choices.

Stop and Give me 5!

This section has, no doubt, stirred up some powerful memories and emotions. Set a timer for 5 minutes and consciously and deliberately relax the tension in your physical body.

Anger is a Choice. Pause.

Yes. Anger is most definitely a choice.

In the midst of a bout of anger it may not appear that way. We get swept along by the high tide of our emotions. We are in it, and we cannot see a way out. But if we pause a moment and notice ourselves, witness what is happening within our body-mind, we can see a brief moment between the trigger and the time when our anger overcomes us.

It may just be a brief pause, not even a full breath, before the wave of anger hits, but it is always there. If you look for it, this gap of time is always there. It is the opportunity when we can choose to pursue angry thoughts or turn toward the action that the anger is asking of us.

Anger is asking for something to change — either within our inner world or our outer world; if anger is present, change is needed.

The mistake that anger makes, again and again, is it demands the **outer world** to change to meet the needs of the **inner world**. That never happens.

True change, lasting change, occurs within us *first*. Only after a change has taken place inside ourselves can our outer world shift. Energetically, it is so.

When we are attached to anger, we emit a deep vibration that keeps the angry things near us and the pleasing things away. Even if we encounter pleasing things, when we are angry, we cannot see them. They might as well not exist, for we cannot let lovely experiences into our world AND grip tightly to anger at the same time. It is one or the other.

Let go of Anger by Understanding it.

"That is nice.", you may say, "Now how the h#ll do I do that?"

It is not the annihilation of anger we are seeking, just the ability to acknowledge the **need** behind the anger. Through the tools in this book, you will develop the ability to recognize when you are **indulging** in anger to avoid doing inner work, and you will gain the ability to **choose** when anger is appropriate and beneficial and when it is destructive.

Banishing anger altogether is not needed or even required. It may not even be possible or wise. Anger is part of our primal sensing apparatus. It helps us avoid and survive danger. To eliminate **all** angry impulses is nearly impossible, but you can do some very important things to decrease random angry moments, decrease your sensitivity to angry thoughts, and to see situations in advance that may trigger your anger, and learn ways of coping or avoiding these triggers altogether.

Mostly, you can easily let go of 90% of your anger with no appreciable negative consequences. You will still have a job; you will still have friends & relatives; you will still interact with people on a daily basis.

This is not about retreating from life. This is about changing your inner self and inner conditions to the extent where the same anger trigger does not affect you. Yes, you will even learn how to drive through rush hour traffic without swearing!

Signs of Spring

Look around the room you are sitting in right now. Find three objects that have, at times, caused or been involved with feelings of anger, irritation, or annoyance. Notice how you feel now about these objects, now that you are not overwhelmed by the moment. Your ability to recognize this difference is a Sign of Spring.

Write this observation in your Signs of Spring journal along with any other signs you have noticed lately.

If You Can Acknowledge It, You Can Change It.

It may seem odd, especially after reading the section on intention, to spend so much time thinking, reading, and focusing on something as unwanted as anger. But I can assure you that whether you acknowledge it or not, anger is part of your deep genetic make-up.

Anger, by its very important and life-saving nature, exists within you. Whether it is expressed or not, it is there.

Acknowledging it, understanding it, and dialoguing with it is a powerful way of ensuring that Anger's needs are met, so you do not need to have a wild and out of control outburst that could damage what you hold dear.

By acknowledging what is true for you, you allow your body-mind to release anger and the pre-conditions for anger before you are actually triggered.

If you acknowledge your current level of anger and then deliberately make a different choice, you give yourself the opportunity to defuse the anger *before* if starts. If you acknowledge anger as part of your meditative practice, you then have the powerful tools and skills necessary to defuse anger in the moment. If you lengthen your moment of clarity between stimulus and response, you can give yourself the gift of those much needed seconds to take a different path and avoid the wreckage that a rage can cause within your body and your life.

By acknowledging and understanding the causes and triggers of your anger, you do not risk increasing your current level of anger. Chances are, if you get angry when you think about your anger, you were probably already pretty angry to begin with.

From a peaceful or calm state, thinking about the underlying causes of your anger will not trigger anger; you remain calm. You can retain your clarity and insight into the reasons behind your anger, and you can delve into the action your anger is needing. From a calm state, you can determine if the first impulsive action that your anger would cause you to make would actually resolve your issue or if it would make things worse.

You get a chance to 'play the scene through to the end'. You can access your wisdom, intellect, and intuitive understanding to predict what would happen if you rushed headlong into the action that anger is prompting you to make.

Sometimes your anger impulses are accurate. Other times, they are not. Only *you* can decide what is the best action to take. Which path would lead to the best outcome for all involved? Which action would give you or others the greatest chance for peace?

Sometimes the action that needs to be taken is uncomfortable, like saying no to excessive demands on your time. The action needed is to say 'no', but how a 'no' is delivered can make or break a friendship, relationship, or job.

Sometimes a 'no' is needed for difficult people, but we say 'no' to the easy people, our children, our friends, the ones who really love us and would understand. We avoid saying 'no' to the people who *need* to hear it the most, our bosses, our co-workers, our obligatory relationships. We avoid confrontation or other people's anger and disappointment by saying 'yes' when we really mean 'no'.

This happens all the time, to the best of us. Don't worry if this sounds like you. Don't worry if you have shouted at a friend when you really wanted to shout at your boss. Don't worry if you shouted at your co-worker if you really wanted to shout at your mate. Don't worry if you shouted at your boss, when you really wanted to shout at your parents.

This is all perfectly normal. It is the rocky ground that needs to be traversed before you can come to the understanding that the problem is not 'them', it is *you*.

Yeah. Ouch! Sorry, but it is true — the common person in all your angry situations is *you*. Even if other people are being a-holes to you, the last thing you want to do is hand them complete power over your emotional state. It is actually an act of tremendous empowerment to take full responsibility for your own emotional state.

You are, at all times, able to control or manage your own emotional state and your reactions and actions. Taking back your power over your emotions is an important step in taking back your power.

Your power is activated when you direct your thoughts and feelings and actions **toward** what you *want* and **away** from what you *don't* want.

When you take full responsibility over your emotional state, you take back your power. The result is 'they' affect you less and less. Ultimately, you find the peace and contentment you were chasing *externally* was residing **within you** the whole time.

Separate the Trigger from the Cause

In the middle of anger it can be very difficult to change your thoughts. Someone says something, or does something you don't like, events don't go your way, things don't go as planned or go at all. You run into obstacles, and your forward momentum is thwarted.

Despite the trigger, the common denominator is you. It is seductive to think, "If 'they' would change or if I could just get what I want, then I would feel better." But it doesn't work that way.

Anger is an internally held emotion. It is triggered by a mixture of biology and psychology. The true cause of anger is rarely the triggered event. We generally assume, when we get angry, the event that triggered the emotion is the same as the cause of the emotion. This is not the case. The cause of anger might be a lack of sleep, being hungry, being confused, or in a vulnerable state.

Our physiology might be primed to elicit an anger response to the most benign of triggers. When we are stressed, our body-minds are flooded with fight or flight information chemicals. It does not take much to set us off. Just like a trigger on a gun, the piece of metal that hammers the bullet, causing an explosive reaction, is not what actually makes the bullet move down the barrel. It is the gunpowder and the construction of the bullet that causes the action. Without gunpowder, the trigger is harmless.

In our bodies, the gunpowder is a complex mix of our biochemistry, stress hormones, previous emotional history, our family of origin issues, and the complexities of our outlook on life on any given day. The cause of the anger may be connected to the trigger, or it could be two completely separate events. Much like how a bad day at work coincides with an outburst of road rage, the trigger event — bad drivers — is separated in time, content, and context from the actual cause — losing the promotion. In order to fully understand our anger, we must be willing to set aside the trigger event and look to the source of our wisdom and the actual action that anger requires of us.

That deeper place, that understands the *actual* cause of our anger, is easier to reach than you might realize. There exists within each of us a deep source of wisdom; some might call it a soul. It is that ageless part of us, the part that impartially witnesses all of the events in our lives and records all of the interconnectedness we may not be aware of. Our soul recalls not only the details of our life experiences, but also the nuances of sensory data surrounding those events. Your soul pays attention to the similarities between people, places, and objects that have importance to us and our purpose. All of this information is within you. It is all accurately recorded and carefully stowed away if you should ever need it.

Turning inward to the vast resources of our souls can shed light on the causes of our anger and guide us towards a positive action that eliminates the need for anger in the first place.

When we look inside, to our souls, we get perspective and peace. Anger is obliterated, and we get very clear guidance on how to take meaningful action that will improve and change our lives.

Releasing Anger Meditation

Take a deep breath.

Find a comfortable seated position.

Rest your arms gently.

Breathe again.

You may be experiencing any number of thoughts and emotions as you begin this meditation.

That is okay. It is perfectly fine. Know that, by just arriving here, you are already beginning to shift.

Just for now, we are going to set aside any heavy or restrictive thoughts or emotions. Take them off, like an old coat.

Let the heaviness come off your shoulders, just for a moment, while we do this meditation.

Acknowledge that you can come back to these thoughts and emotions if you need them later.

But for right now, you will pack them away, just like an old winter coat. Fold it carefully and place it inside a large cedar chest.

This chest will keep whatever issue is troubling you safe while you journey. Your guide, or your guardian angel, will watch over the chest while you continue on.

Breathe deeply. Breathe fully.

Before you is a beautiful archway in a grassy meadow.

Beyond the archway, you see a path worn into the dirt, winding up a low, grass-covered hill.

The path beckons you forward and as you walk beneath the arch you feel a shift in the weather.

The wind is blowing and swirling around you. As you walk up the hill, you find that the wind is beginning to blow stronger and stronger. The wind pushes against you.

This wind is your resistance. The force of the wind pushes against you as you push against it. It is clear. Pushing does not work here. The more resistance you have, the stronger the wind blows.

Take a moment now. With your eyes gently closed, feel how strong the wind is for you.

Now, take a deep breath and allow the wind to push through you. The wind goes right through you, and as it does, it loses some of its energy. It gets just a little easier to walk. It softens, just a little bit.

Take a moment now to breathe. Let the wind go through you, and take a step further up the path. Breathe, let the wind go through you, and take another step.

Continue this way until you reach the top of the hill. Just breathe, let it flow, let it go, let it go through you, and walk steadily, step by step, to the top.

You may experience different thoughts and emotions as you walk up the hill. That is okay. Just notice how strongly the wind is blowing and then let the wind go right through you.

Breathe and let it go.

Breathe and let it go.

Continue on, until you reach the top.

As you reach the top of the hill, you see a great circle of stones. In the centre of the circle, there is a beautiful fountain.

At the very top of the fountain there is a very large, clear crystal sphere.

The sunlight shines through the crystal, and you see multi-coloured rainbows and lights, deep within the crystal.

The crystal sphere glows as if lit from within. It seems to emit its own light. Within the light, you see a figure moving.

This is your divine guardian, the steward of your soul, and the caretaker of your book in the hall of records, where every detail of your life has been written.

All of the connections and interconnections with everyone you have ever known is written in your own life book. Your guardian knows all of this and more.

Your divine guardian emerges from the crystal and walks toward you. They greet you warmly and ask you to sit and chat with them.

You can ask them anything you like. They have deep and ancient knowledge that is guided by the compassionate nature of the Universe.

Your guardian can share any information that will support you in your journey towards peace. They know exactly what will help you let go of the causes of anger and replace them with peace, calm love, joy, and wisdom.

You may be shown different parts of the movie of your life, you may have a conversation; you may just sit still in the presence of this divine being and receive healing. Whatever happens is right for you. Spend a few moments now receiving this kind information.

Thank your divine guardian for their wise and kind information.

Your divine guardian, the keeper of your book of wisdom, says good-bye and returns to the centre of the crystal.

Take a moment to absorb the beauty of this place. Notice, now, the softness of the breeze. Notice, now, the beautiful sunshine, all around you. Sunshine filling you. Sunshine cleansing you. You are filled with light now. You feel so light now. You are light.

Now, walk back down the path, easy, relaxed, and free. Walk back to the archway. As you walk under the archway, you notice that the sunny and beautiful weather has followed you.

Thank your guardian for their wise guidance. Take a deep breath. Come back fully into your body. Wiggle your fingers and your toes. Give yourself a hug and a stretch. Your meditation is done.

Sharing Circle

Spend the next 5 minutes writing about your experience in the meditation. Write down the wisdom your guides and angels had for you, your insight into your problem, and its natural solution.

If you are working through the book in a group, share your experiences now.

Self Care & Love

Letting Go Of Anger Is a Profound Act of Self-Love

Letting go of anger is a huge act of self-love. While others around you may benefit from your improved demeanour, YOU are the one who truly reaps the benefits.

Self-care and self-love occur at a deep level the moment you let anger or an angry thought go. You need not ever get all the way to feeling completely peaceful. It is enough to just have the desire to change, and the change will occur.

Letting go of anger is heavy work, so it is important to take some time to lighten up.

Humour is a powerful antidote to anger. If you can laugh, even at something unrelated, you activate very powerful resources at your disposal. If anger is a primal state, triggered by a threat, laughter is as close to its opposite as you can get.

If you watch stand-up comedians, there is absolutely no subject that is off limits. Once a joke can be made, however, healing can begin. Now, of course, there is huge variation in what is funny to each person. Personally, I am not a fan of mean, racist, sexist, or practical jokes. I tend to prefer witty, life commentary humour, or physical comedy. Monty Python and Tina Fey are some of my favorites.

In the end, it does not matter **what** makes you laugh; it just matters **that** you laugh.

Just as anger releases a cascade of neurotransmitters and hormones, so does laughter. Laughing is a uniquely human thing we do. Laughing changes our physiology, decreases cortisol and stress hormones, and quickly shifts our perspective on life in a manner of minutes.

Just for Today — Laugh!

Just for today, find the humour in the moment you are in. Look around and find a new and unexpected way of viewing things. Read a funny book, watch a favorite comedy, call up your funniest friend, make silly faces in the mirror. Have a belly laugh today. Seek laughter.

If you are a bit stuck and don't already have a list of your funniest movies or books, check out laughter yoga. Laughter yoga originated in India and is a series of goofy exercises that people use to laugh. They often start out with fake laughter, but the laughter soon becomes real, especially when done in a group.

Check out some videos online, and you will see what I mean. I have tried Laughter yoga at home, and I can honestly say it is one of the best ab workouts I have ever done!

Just for today...deliberately lower your physiological stress by having a good belly laugh.

Intuition

Your Intuition can get rid of Anger before It Starts

Our intuition is a deeply ingrained system that evolved in order to predict the behaviour of predators. If you can sense what a lion is thinking and feeling, you can then avoid them **before** they pounce. You get early warning signals in many different ways before a threat becomes real. Anger is a last resort. Intuition is the early warning system that keeps us from harm.

Our intuition is part of this survival sensory system and encompasses all of the various ways information can be received, energetic, visual, tactile, and scent. Many of these signals may be beyond the realm of our conscious awareness. All of the information we can receive in any given second far exceeds our ability to process it. If we leave our intuition as an unconscious process, we tend to get vague feelings of uneasiness, a weird, empty feeling in the pit of the stomach, or 'the creeps'. While this level of intuitive information might be sufficient to guide you, it can be too easily overridden by your logical mind or your need to keep other people happy and comfortable. Without activating and using our intuitive knowledge, we can easily misread our signals or ignore them entirely.

Bringing our intuitive knowledge to conscious awareness strengthens its signals over time and also improves its accuracy. At first, if you haven't used your intuition regularly, or if you smother its signals, you may not receive clear messages.

The messages you could get at first could be vague sensa-tions, a vague feeling in the pit of your stomach or so on. These signals from your intuition could be very subtle and difficult to distinguish from the background noise of your mind. If you have a very active and chattering mind, then sometimes the intuitive signals get lost before you become aware of them.

You are able to receive accurate intuitive guidance directly from Source on any subject you are interested in, with only your open heart and mind as your tools. There is nothing too big or too little that escapes the mind of God/Divine/Universe. You can access this deeper wisdom for any topic, at any time. You can access this place yourself, without any other person or psychic or oracle deck to help you.

Don't get me wrong, I love oracle decks, runes, and other intuitive resources. They can be wonderful means of accessing and verifying your intuition. Great as external sources are, I really want you to begin practicing using your whole body-mind as your oracle.

Your most reliable and convenient method of accessing your intuition is your own body-mind. For the purposes of this book, I want you to begin to listen to your body in a deeper way than you may be used to. By getting you to access your wisdom in your body, you can begin to hone your intuitive signals, so you will eventually get clear and unmistakable signals.

Developing this level of deep, clear, and accurate messages from your higher guidance is invaluable. Ultimately, we all crave this level of connection to our inner resources. Not only is this level of dialogue possible for you, having a clear intuition is very useful in life. Listening to your intuition can de-fuse anger and its triggers before it even gets going.

Using your intuition to guide your life results in far fewer angry episodes and a general ease throughout your day. Everything just goes better when you follow Divine Guidance.

By strengthening your intuition, you can begin to make better decisions for yourself. Over time, your intuition will naturally guide you away from situations and people that could cause you harm or trigger anger. You will find you just aren't around as many annoying people anymore. But the real shift is within *you*. Use your intuition as your life compass, and it steers you towards calm water and safe harbours every time, without fail.

Use your Intuition!

Make small decisions, based on your intuitive guidance. Unless you have a well-developed intuition, it may be difficult to distinguish between signals of fear and limitation from your ego and the ease and expansion from your Source.

The coolest thing about intuition is you do not need to leave your logic and reason behind to be an intuitive person living a Divinely guided life. Far from it! Intuition can always be combined with the power of your intellect to guide the best choices for your life. It is not an either/or scenario. Use both the wisdom of your heart and the knowledge of your intellect to discern if an intuitive impulse is right for you.

Be wary of the impulse to abandon your life on a whim. Usually, the 'abandon all thought and run away from my life' impulses are a symptom of numbing and avoidance, rather than originating from a deep desire for change. While it can be cathartic to quit your job, move to a different city, and leave your lover, ultimately, *you* are still *you*. Your problems will find you wherever you go. You take them with you.

So yes, you may have tremendous changes in your outer life as you embark on this journey toward happiness. But the changes you are really wanting and needing are *internal*. Start there.

You want to *feel* better. You want to *feel* happy. You want to *feel* free. You want to *feel* powerful. All of those are *feelings*. And feelings can be transformed almost overnight, without losing all the hard work that has gotten you to this point in your life.

So please, start small. Choose decisions that are simple, like soup or salad, left or right, apple or orange. Once you're getting clear and reliable signals, you can expand using your intuition to guide more significant decisions.

For me, it took me a while to get to the point where I was able to trust my intuition on larger decisions, about 5 or 6 years. Now, I use my intuition in everything I do. I consider my intuition to be just as valuable as my sight or hearing.

Intuition is a 'sense'. Use ALL of your senses!

Just for Today — Notice the Ease

Pay attention to the ease or resistance in your body as you go about your day. When you are following your intuitive guidance, you feel relaxation in your body. Your shoulders drop, you feel good. You have perfect timing and are in the right place at the right time. When you are resisting your intuitive guidance, you feel resistance, you feel tension, you get blocked at every turn, and things just don't work out, no matter how much effort you put in.

Keep a record of your experiences. Track your outcome of the decisions you make with your intuition. When you follow your intuitive guidance, take a moment to scan your whole body from scalp to toes.

Where do you feel your intuition most strongly in your body? What parts tighten? Which parts relax? Do you see a glow around objects that are 'right'? Do you feel a heaviness or lightness in objects you are choosing between? Lightness usually signals a 'yes' and heaviness usually signals a 'no'.

Spend time getting reacquainted with your body and its signals. The more you use your intuition, the stronger it gets. As your intuition grows, watch as your anger and irritation begin to dissipate. Practice tuning in to your intuition every day for the best results.

Just for today... would you like an apple or an orange? :)

Stop and Give me 5!

Notice the level of anger in your body right now, in this moment. No need to dig it up, just honestly assess how much anger you are carrying with you, right now. For the next 5 minutes, use the ocean of your breath to gently wash away your anger. Each breath in gathers the anger; each breath out washes the anger out to sea.

Visualize your anger floating away from you and out to sea. Allow the vast wisdom of the ocean to transform, transmute, and reduce the anger until all that is left is calm and relaxation.

Rate your anger again after the meditation. Write down your experience in your journal.

Signs of Spring

Do you notice the times when anger is a choice?

Whether you fall into the experience of anger or not, being able to notice the moment of choice is a Sign of Spring.

Write down any moments when you were able to witness your anger and its triggers or deeper causes.

It takes incredible skill to deconstruct even one angry moment. Honour yourself for this huge achievement. Even if you have not noticed the moment of choice within your anger, honour yourself for getting to this page. You are showing up. And showing up is the start of change, a sure sign of spring!

Affirmation Ladder

Okay.

I love using affirmations. I really do.

But I also know there are times when repeating these positive statements about peace and love are just downright annoying. If you are one of the people who feels like affirmations don't work for you, it might be because the affirmation you are using is too different from what you usually think and feel.

Affirmations are just positive statements you repeat, so you can deliberately change your thoughts. Affirmation Ladders give you a way to honestly appraise where you are, right now, and give you a statement that will ease you upward towards peace.

With the Affirmation Ladders in this book, you can gradually work your way up to a more and more positive statement, with minimal emotional turbulence that might stall your progress. The Affirmation Ladders allow you to assess where you are and then use the affirmation that will nudge you, ever so gently, up the ladder to the next rung.

For each of the Reiki Ideals, you get a new Affirmation Ladder. Check out the appendix at the back of the book for a handy place to look them all up. You can also download your own snazzy reference sheet for free at genevarobins.com/affirmationladders.

Release Anger Bit By Bit with Affirmations

Releasing anger may seem a bit of a backwards affirmation, especially after reading the Intention Chapter, because you are pointed towards what is unwanted in your life. That is true, to some extent, because you want to describe and visualize a life **without** uncontrolled anger. You want to begin visualizing a life of peace, contentment, and happiness as soon as you can.

The trouble with jumping straight to an affirmation, like "My life is peaceful and joyous", is if you are in the grips of anger, an affirmation like that will feel like a lie. It is most likely that a strongly positive affirmation, when you are feeling strongly negative, will just frustrate or enrage you even further.

It doesn't work all that well to reduce or diffuse the angry moment you are in.

The solution is quite simple. Work your way up to a strongly positive affirmation by a series of little steps.

Begin by rating the level of anger in your body, right now. Scan your body and look for tension. Feel the **truth** for you in this moment.

Rank your anger on a scale from 0 to 10. Zero is feeling completely content, happy, and at peace; ten is feeling blind rage, as angry as you have ever felt in your life, literally howling with rage. A six or seven would be feeling pissed off or hot under the collar, the muttering under your breath or snarky remark stage. A two or three would be something like irritation or annoyance.

What number are you at, right now?

Take the first response that pops into your head. There is no right or wrong here. No one is judging you or giving you a grade.

While a ten is unpleasant to feel for any length of time, it is brief and can be overcome. At the same time, a score of zero does not make you 'good'. It can also be briefly experienced. Anger comes and goes in response to life experiences and our reaction to them. Again, the problem is not with **having** anger; the problem is with **holding on** to anger.

Just answer honestly, and you will get the best results.

If you are having a really hard time ranking your anger level, read through the list of affirmations in the Letting Go of Anger Affirmation Ladder. The one that resonates the most with you is the one you need.

Letting Go of Anger Affirmation Ladder

0	Peace becomes me. I am peaceful, joyful, and loving. I understand my true nature is joy.
1	Love is everywhere I look. It is all around me all the time.
2	Love, peace and understanding are always available to me. Each breath I breathe is a new chance.
3	Peace is all around me, right around the corner. I know where to look to find the answers I need.
4	Breathing in, I am love. Breathing out, I have time. Every breath offers me a chance to change.
5	I take the time to know myself. I know that I am loving and lovable.
6	I embrace my feelings with love and acceptance. I know I can sort out the real issue below it all.
7	All my emotions are wise teachers. I accept them as the lessons they are. Clarity is all around me.
8	I am feeling angry and it is okay. I know I can use the energy released by this angry experience for positive change.
9	I am feeling angry. Although I am angry right now, I know this feeling will pass and I will get clarity on the real issue.
10	I am feeling really angry right now. Absolutely furious. Even though I am so overcome with anger and rage right now, I am still a good person.

Just for Today — Affirm your Way to Peace

Test these affirmations out, daily, for a few days. See which ones 'zing' — which ones really resonate with you and help you release anger. If you can nudge your level up by just one level, it is a major win.

Spend time hanging out with each affirmation before moving on to the next, lowered numbered one. Make sure you really *feel* the affirmation to be true before leaping ahead.

You can repeat the affirmations while looking in a mirror to get huge benefits. The mirror reflects the truth. If you cringe while repeating an affirmation, try going one up or down to feel your way toward one that resonates as truth. You can use sticky notes or dry erase marker on your mirror, so you get a daily reminder to repeat the new thought pattern.

Repeat the affirmations out loud. It may feel slightly uncomfortable at first, but that just means you are changing. When you use your voice, you are creating a physical wave of sound. Sound waves are matter, so you are literally changing matter every time you speak. When you say positive words, you reap positive rewards. The changes happen faster the more you practice and the more dedication you invest in the practice.

Take the time to get the resonance before you move on up to the next affirmation up the ladder. By slowing down, you will actually move through your anger faster. Wait until you feel ease and relaxation with the affirmation before going on to the next one.

Congratulations! You are doing really well! Keep going!

Just for today... affirm your progress towards peace.

Sharing Circle

Spend the next 5 minutes writing about your experience with the Peace/Anger Affirmation Ladder.

How do you feel now, compared to how you felt before the affirmation practice?

*What would change in your life if you started using the ladder
every day?*

Practice

It is to your benefit to fully understand the anatomy of your
anger, its triggers, and causes before going too far ahead. As
uncomfortable as it may be, exploring anger for the purpose of
transformation is far better than leaving it to an unconscious
process that can sneak up on you and dominate your life and
experience.

Understanding and acknowledging a pattern is a key to
releasing anything that is uncomfortable. Honour your truth
and your experience fully.

It is okay to be angry.

It is okay to be peaceful.

Wherever you are is just fine.

Cause versus Trigger

So, how do you tease apart the difference between a *cause*
of anger and the *trigger* of anger? Well, wonder no more!

A *trigger* of anger is the event, precisely *before* the anger
occurred. The trigger may or may not have *anything* to do
with the real *cause* of your anger. The trouble with anger, in
its uncontrollable and unconscious state, is we often mistake
the trigger as the *cause* of our anger, when it rarely is.

We can spend a lot of time trying to change, control, or fix
the triggers of anger in our lives, but next to no time defusing
the actual *cause* of the anger.

The trouble with trying to solve anger by addressing the
triggers is if you are able to fix one, twelve more take its place.
Until you can solve, or at least become aware of, the real

reason behind the anger and its cause, you will be caught in an endless loop.

The causes of anger are nearly always internal. Feelings of vulnerability, danger (real or perceived), lack of love or attention, or a vital need being threatened are common causes of anger. A vital need is one that is, or feels like, it is necessary to our very survival.

A vital need is physical safety, safety of our children and loved ones, protection of our homes and belongings, and our basic needs for survival like food, water, and shelter. Of course, people need far more than physical sustenance and protection from threats and harm to truly survive.

People are hardwired to form communities, families, tribes, and towns. We naturally seek each other out. For much of our human history, our survival depended on being in protective relationships with other humans. These relationships, even primitive ones, kept us safe and ensured our survival. Threats to an important relationship is a very common cause of anger.

It is funny, though; our anger at someone close is often because we are afraid to lose them, not because they left the toothpaste tube out or put back an empty milk carton in the fridge!

We can undermine the very relationship we fear losing, by not knowing the true internal cause of our anger.

That Dang Carton

Let's ponder this scene... you open the fridge to find a pitiful slop of milk left in the carton. Instantly, your blood boils over.

"How insensitive! How rude! What an inconsiderate #!#@#!"

Okay, awesome! Pause there! You just noticed that you are furious! Excellent!

Now, notice that you could measure the pause between the discovery of the empty carton and the full flung, swept away to Angry Town, expression of anger in micro-seconds.

Huzzah! You are doing so well!

Even though brief, the moment between trigger and anger is there. With time and practice, your awareness of this pause can lengthen the actual time you have to make a different choice.

The pause is always there. Always. And in that pause, if you have enough time, you can sneak in this question to yourself before your anger runs away with you.

"What is this *really* about?"

Look for the answer to this question within. Know that there is some deep need that your primal part of your brain feels is not being met, so you leap towards anger as self-preservation.

You could fight your way out. And sometimes, you may need to. But here, with the only threat being we might have to have toast for breakfast or we might need to make an extra stop on the way home, chances are we do not need to put up our dukes to survive.

It is an empty milk jug, not a loaded weapon or a jungle cat.

Some part of us knows this, even as we slide down the slippery slope to full out tantrum. We are maybe being ridiculous here or blowing things out of proportion, which is true. But keep in mind, this is just the trigger.

This is not about milk.

So what is the vital need here?

Maybe it is about not feeling respected or cared for. Maybe it is fears about money or not having enough. Maybe you have had some upsetting news at work, and you are worried about being laid off. Maybe you are just hangry, so hungry you get angry at the mere thought of a delay in getting food.

The action the anger really needs you to take could be having a heart to heart with your partner about your troubles, or you may need to update your resume, or maybe you need a good night's sleep. Maybe you need to reset your stress levels, so you are not primed for that unconscious fight or flight response.

Whatever the case, explore the internal causes of your anger and begin exploring internal solutions.

You will be amazed at how much of your anger is really about something entirely different from the trigger and how much of it stems from an *internal* need you can meet yourself.

Just for Today — Notice the Pause

Note your anger when it arises and gently turn your attention *away* from the initial trigger event and ask yourself: 'If the true source of my feelings of anger in this moment were within *me*, what vital need do I have that is demanding my attention? Which vital need is the true cause of this angry episode?'

Just gently explore this question. It is important not to shift blame for the anger at yourself.

It is okay to be angry!

It is okay to be livid!

It is okay to be enraged!

Know you have the ability, right now, in this moment, to understand what vital need needs to be met and by taking *action* when you are calmer, to address that need you can immediately change your patterns of holding on to anger.

Try these steps to work through your anger:

1. **Pause.** As soon as you notice your anger levels rising, stop what you are doing and become physically still. Look for the pause, the space between trigger and anger.

2. **Calm.** Breathe. Use meditation or affirmations to take the edge off of your anger response. This allows you to add more space to the mix, so you can act methodically, rather than reacting unconsciously.

3. **Cause.** When your anger levels have dropped a bit, ask yourself what the deeper cause of the anger might be. Where is the true source of this feeling? Be willing to look beyond the immediate situation to the larger scope of your life.

4. **Action.** If you received a clear answer to the true cause of your anger in the last step, then spend some time in meditation asking your higher self what is the action that needs to be taken and the timing of that action. It is always best to take your action when you are at a lower level of anger. That way, you are not just taking a knee-jerk, compulsive reaction; you are giving yourself the space you need to make a plan for the best action for your body, mind, and spirit.

Just for today...understand the cause and notice the pause.

CHAPTER FIVE:

Letting Go of Worry

Faith is the bird that feels the light when the dawn is still dark.
  ~ Rabindranath Tagore

Hello Worry, my old friend!

I am well acquainted with worry. Are you?

Letting go of worry is the second Reiki Ideal. While anger can feel empowering at times, if not exhausting, worry wears you down and destroys any sense of power you may have had. Worry is pure trickery. Worry fools us into believing that, if we keep our minds active and filled with emotion over a certain topic, then we are actually ***doing*** something about it. Let me be clear, worry never accomplishes anything, ever.

Worry hinders any action on the subject you are worrying about and dams up creativity and awareness. You cannot see the solution to the problem; in worry, there is only the problem.

Worry Defined

Worry is an offshoot of the fear group of emotions. Fear is a very primal emotion. Fear's ultimate purpose is to alert us to danger. Anger would then, naturally, accompany fear in our protective response. Fear identifies the threat; anger moves us out of the way, or neutralizes the threat.

Fear is felt the instant before flight, in the fight or flight response. Fear is the jolt of adrenaline and cortisol we get juiced with, so our bodies are capable of remarkable feats of strength, agility, and speed that keep us safe. In a dangerous situation, fear and its corresponding flight are protective. But, this same response, held over a long period of time, wears down the body-mind.

Stress, from a multitude of causes, can keep us in this uncharted fear-state for days at a time, but the toll it takes on the body is terrible. We literally burn ourselves out.

Fear, just like anger, can have a highly protective role in our lives. It is not needed, nor wise, to try to remove fear from one's life. But fear, once activated, can keep going long after the initial impulse, stimulus, is gone. We can become primed for fear, just as we can become primed for anger. The stress state we have continually elevates our stress hormones. We have fear on a hair trigger. It becomes easier to stay in fear and to respond to the slightest threat with an unwarranted level of fear.

Worry is connected to fear. Worry happens when we perceive a threat or danger to our, or a loved one's, well-being. The main difference with worry is it is connected to situations we feel helpless to change. Worry avoids change. It blocks creative problem solving, and it derails our hope or belief that we, or our loved ones, are capable and strong.

Worry's twin sister is anxiety. Anxiety and worry are nearly synonymous, with anxiety, perhaps, being the extreme end of the worry spectrum.

Worry is a constantly busy mind that continually repeats imagery and thoughts of fear and anxiety. Worry usually is connected to situations where it appears we have little control in the outcome. Helplessness and hopelessness are closely connected to worry. Since our minds are so *busy* when we are worried, we can be fooled into thinking we are *doing* something about a problem. Worrying does *nothing*, absolutely *nothing*, to solve or resolve our problems. Worry's best advice is to freeze, stay still, do not move, do not act, do not change, stay stuck. Staying stuck in a problem does not solve it, ever.

It Is Okay To Let Go Of Worry

Worry is *different* from concern or attentiveness to our problems. A life free from worry is not one where we insulate ourselves from our problems or bury our heads in the sand. Letting go of worry does not mean we abandon our jobs, forfeit our responsibilities, or run away from home. It means we stay rooted and grounded in ourselves; in the midst of our problems, we turn our gaze toward hope and away from fear.

We start searching for the solution, instead of being mired in the problem. Letting go of worry requires us to get acquainted with our vulnerability and learn to find our roots and stay grounded in the midst of chaos and uncertainty.

Worries often crop up when we are faced with a problem we don't know how to solve that might occur in the future or did occur in the past. If you observe yourself carefully, we rarely worry about what is happening right now. Even if we are anxious in a particular activity, the anxiety tends to be connected to future outcomes or other people's perceptions.

You begin thinking repetitive thoughts like these:

What will they think about me?

What ARE they thinking of me?

What will happen if I fail?

What will happen WHEN I fail?

Worry exists if three conditions are met:

1. lack of faith in our own or another's capability to manage our problems;
2. being overly concerned with another's opinions or emotions; or
3. preoccupation with the past or future.

All of these are rooted in a lack of self-love and self-confidence.

Even when we worry about another, what we are really worrying about is our doubt *we* can handle a negative outcome in the life of someone we love. At best, worry depletes resources that could be used to solve problems and support people in their growth and development. At worst, worry becomes toxic, stifling our (and another's) freedom to grow, change, and take well-placed risks that allow us to live our true life purpose.

Think back to your life 5 years ago. What was your greatest worry then? How much does that same issue affect you today? Chances are high that the majority of your worries back then are not even an issue now. The tiny fraction of worries that are still an issue now, are likely the only ones that probably deserved your attention at all. Even for that small percentage of long-term worries, ask yourself if **worrying** actually solved them.

What *did* solve those problems?

A change in perception? A new resource was accessed? A new skill needed? An action was taken? Did you get help from a trusted person? Did you let God/the Divine/Source Energy help you?

Maybe all you did was resign yourself that the worry or trouble was, ultimately, unsolvable and made peace with *what is,* instead of struggling against it. Maybe you just got distracted by another stream of worries, which you also have since resolved.

When you let go of worry, you are not being irresponsible or careless. You are actually doing the best thing you can for yourself and everyone around you. Resolving worry frees up tremendous resources, so you can focus on making real and lasting changes in your life.

Facing Worry helped me Conquer a Huge Goal

I tend to be really driven to achieve. I am, after all, a recovering perfectionist. I stalled out in writing my Master's thesis for over two years due to my worry that my committee would fail me. I had worked so hard during my research. It had to be perfect, and I knew (or thought I knew) nothing I wrote would be good enough.

My worry paralyzed me. I had the worst case of writer's block I have ever experienced.

Worry was ever present in those days. Whether or not I was writing, I was gripped with worry. I felt like I was both frozen in ice, incapable of moving, and at the same time a feeling of being consumed with a smoldering ember of regret and recrimination. Trapped, unable to move, unable to run, but wanting to burst through the cage of my life experience.

If I was the type of person who had trouble with commitment, I would have run away and left town. But I knew if had run away from my Master's thesis, the regret would have just chased me all over the world.

I clung to worry though, because I felt if I stopped worrying, I would just give up and not complete my degree at all. In the past, I had used worry as a motivational tool to whip myself into high performance, whenever my schooling or career demanded a deadline be met.

I was terrified to let go of worry, because I didn't trust myself to complete a task without it. In the end, though, the only way I could write at all was to completely surrender the outcome, completely surrender the past, and completely focus on the present moment.

I could not think any further ahead than the next sentence. I had to remain rooted in the NOW, because I would become paralyzed if I let my mind wander in the least. If I thought about the past, I would beat myself up about how long it had taken me and how little I had accomplished. If I thought about the future, I would think about failing the thesis defense and not being able to answer the most basic questions. If I only allowed myself to think about just the next word and the next sentence, I could actually write. It was the only thing that worked.

I finished my 365-page manuscript in less than 6 weeks. I powered through it by deliberately focusing on the present moment in every moment of the day. No matter what I was doing, whether it was writing, stopping for lunch, spending time with my young family, or nursing my son, I was completely focused on what I was doing in each moment.

I deliberately forced myself not to indulge in worry. I just allowed myself to rest, eat, sleep, and write whenever I was doing each of those things. When I was writing, that was all I was doing, writing. When I was eating lunch, that was all I was doing, eating lunch. Every activity, I gave my complete focus. If my focus shifted, then I did that new activity.

I was remarkably productive, and what I produced had merit. In the end, I not only passed my thesis defense, but several committee members ranked my thesis in the top 10 to 30% of theses they had reviewed. Huzzah!

The relief in completing such a huge goal was enormous. I was so happy to have persevered and finished my degree. All it took was a refusal to waste effort worrying and a dogged focus on the present moment.

It was mindfulness in action. It was the best possible experience for me to learn how harmful and non-productive worry was for me and how important and powerful mindfulness can be.

Mindfulness Dissolves Worry

Being mindful of one's thoughts and activities is hugely effective in handling worry. Mindfulness meditation is a practice that focuses the mind on only this present moment.

Right now, you are reading this sentence.

There!

You just did it! You were mindful!

There!

You did it again! Awesome job you!

In all seriousness, mindfulness is a hugely important technique in resolving worry. Worry tends to be exclusively focused in the past or the future. Very rarely does worry actually concern what is happening in the present moment. The present is the **only** time we can do anything about the situation.

Even if we cannot change a situation we are in, we can still change our feelings and thoughts about it. We can turn towards hope. We can ask for Divine intervention. We can surrender the problem entirely. We can brainstorm solutions. All of those things happen **now**, in the present.

Remaining focused in the present moment is a feat of enormous strength and courage. A lot of energy is tied up in worry that can make it really difficult to think about what is happening right now.

Worried thoughts produce and attract more worried thoughts, until every moment is spent worrying. You can even worry about how much you are worrying and worry that, if you stopped worrying, all hell would break loose. Honestly, the worst thing that would happen if you stopped worrying would be exactly **nothing**. Worry does not solve your problems. It only keeps your mind so busy it is **impossible** to solve your problems.

Staying stuck in worry is a guarantee of a poor outcome, or at least, worse than it could be. Not only will you be miserable along the way, but even if everything works out okay, you are often so exhausted you can't properly enjoy it.

Trust me. I speak from experience. Worry, fear, and anxiety used to be my everyday experience. It got to be so normal to wake up in near terror every morning; I rarely had a moment when I could take a deep breath and relax. Every morning, I would hide under the covers, hugging myself, until the grip of anxiety would ease enough so I could get out of bed. My body-mind was constantly flooded with adrenaline and cortisol. Everything I did took effort and force to happen because I was so gripped with fear.

That pattern began to change for me when I discovered yoga, meditation, and later, Reiki. The mindful techniques in all three practices allowed me to get brief glimpses into what a settled and still mind could look like. A still mind does not look like a mind devoid of all thought. Rather, it is learning to slow the unwanted, rampaging, worry thoughts, and instead, focus on feelings and thoughts of ease, joy, and happiness.

The Present Moment is the Point Of Change

One requirement for worry is the preoccupation with the future or the past. A chronic worrier spends nearly all of their time in any moment BUT the present one. When you focus on the present moment, worry eases almost by magic.

Keep returning to the present moment. The events in the present, even physical or emotional pain, are not minimized or banished with this practice, but rather, they and given space to simply be. Deliberately surrender your troubles and just allow them space to remain, shift, or relax on their own accord. Become mindful of the present moment, and in that moment, you can relax.

If you can shift your focus, if for only a moment, to the present, you immediately shift worry to a more positive state. *Worry and mindfulness cannot co-exist.* By entering a state of mindfulness, you immerse yourself in the present moment.

The present moment is the only time you can actually change anything or do anything. Even when we prepare for a future task, the 'preparing' is done in the present. When the moment of the task arrives, we execute the task in the *present*. Thinking of only the past or future immediately robs us of our inherent power and creates unnecessary anxiety.

Meditation

The meditative practice for this chapter is, drumroll... mindfulness!

The simplest mindful technique is very easy. All you need to do is ask yourself these two questions:

"Where am I?"

"What am I doing?"

Your answer is best kept to a very simple one or two word response. Repeat these questions for a 5-minute meditation, or you can also use these questions any time worry pops up. They will instantly derail your worry train and give you a chance to catch your breath.

For me, right now, these are my answers.

Where am I? — In my living room.

What am I doing? — Writing.

Where am I? — In my room.

What am I doing? — Writing.

Where am I? — In my house.

What am I doing? — Sitting.

Where am I? — On earth.

What am I doing? — Breathing.

As you can see, you can choose to change the answer to keep your mind engaged on the present, or you can repeat the same answer for 5 minutes straight. Just go with your first response. Keep it simple. Keep it quick. Repeat these questions to yourself in a singsongy way. It is a chant. It has a rhythm. Find yours.

Find the rhythm of the moment you are in and just answer these very basic questions for the duration of your meditation; you may notice you will begin to feel relaxation in your body and mind slowly replace whatever state you were in before you started.

You may feel a lightness and expansion after a session, though that is not typically the goal. The goal is to focus solely on the present. It is practice for a living a fully conscious life. It is practice for achieving a balanced approach to your problems. You learn the skills of staying steady in the midst of chaos through the practice of mindfulness.

If you are able to achieve mastery over your own chaotic thoughts, handling the outer chaos in your busy and bustling life is a piece of cake.

Releasing Worry Meditation

Breathe gently.

Settle in and gently relax your eyes.

Acknowledge that, over the next few minutes, you will be deliberately pressing the pause button on whatever is held in the mind.

Whatever racing, anxious, troublesome, or distracting thought might be in your mind right now, just press pause.

It is okay. It is okay to set this aside for a moment. You can always come back to it later.

Just for now, pause.

You are not abandoning your issue; you are not being uncaring; you are just merely pausing.

The purpose of this entire meditation practice is to drop your heart rate, allow your body-mind to rest, and to recuperate your physiological setting. You are deliberately dropping all your levels back to resting.

Do this now.

Consciously slow your breathing, still your movements, and allow your heart rate to slow to resting.

Breathe in... 1...2...3...4...

Breathe out...1...2...3...4...

Breathe in... 1...2...3...4...5...

Breathe out...1...2...3...4...5...

Breathe in... 1...2...3...4...5...6...
Breathe out...1...2...3...4...5...6...
Breathe in... 1...2...3...4...5...6...7...
Breathe out...1...2...3...4...5...6...7...

Before you is an instrument panel, just like one you would see at a recording studio. A giant board of sliding switches. There is a slider for your heart rate, for your cortisol and stress hormones, even sliders for each and every thought you had as you started this meditation. You can safely adjust these levels to a soothing and comfortable place.

Do this now.

Turn down the volume on your stress hormones. Let them drop to resting.

There. That is right.

Now, let's turn down the volume on the unhelpful thoughts. Maybe even mute them, you see, the button right there.

Now, let's increase the slider for peacefulness. Yes. There it is.

Increase faith. You've got it now.

Oh look. There is the one for gratitude. Increase that all the way.

Now, yes. There is worthiness. That one also goes way up.

Oh and valuable. You are valuable, so that goes up too.

Oh look! There is a double slider. Kindness for you and kindness for others, make sure they are equal. Push them right to the top.

Wonderful.

Now, step into the sound booth. Notice how quiet it is here. Safe. Serene. Listening. Observing. The mike is on.

Say the word 'Here'
Say the word 'Now'
Here
Now
Here

Now

Here

Now

I lere

Now

Here

Now

Here

Now

Here

Now

Here

Now

Here

Now

Here

Now

Here

Now

Here

Now

Here

Now

Breathe deeply.

Breathe gently.

Give yourself a hug and a stretch. Your meditation is done.

Sharing Circle

Spend the next 5 minutes writing about your experience in the meditation.

What happened to your worry levels?

Did you pick up the worries you set aside?

Did you have any realizations of how to handle the situations you typically worry about?

If you are working through the book in a group, share your experiences now.

Stop and Give me 5!

Yes. That is right. Right now.

Meditate.

Right.

Now.

Wherever you are NOW. What time is it? Now.

What are you doing right now? :)

Oh! That is right! You are meditating!

Self Care & Love

Worry takes its toll on us. It is like walking around with sand in our shoes. At first, it doesn't bother us too much, just a little uncomfortable. But soon, all the worries pile up and pile on. We get sore; we get raw; we get weary. The physical and mental toll is very high. We literally wear ourselves out.

The blessing is that worry is a choice. We actually choose to worry. We nurture worry in ourselves and others. We mistake worry for care, compassion, and action.

Because worry is really nothing more than a mental habit, we can form new habits. We can replace our old way of thinking and being with a more healthful, more helpful mode of existence.

Chances are, there are times when worry has been low or nearly gone for you. Even a brief decrease in worry is a cause for celebration.

I used to experience these low worry states only on vacation. When I was travelling, I had to keep my wits about me. I couldn't afford to be distracted with worry. There was too much to see, do, negotiate, and translate. Travelling forced me into the present moment and worry vanished.

Perhaps going on vacation is the same for you. Maybe it is something else. Perhaps it is engaging in a pleasurable hobby, running, sports, crafts, knitting, fishing, so forth.

Activities where you are engaged in the task at hand, that are fun, that require your concentration and focus to do well, these activities can derail worry and anxiety. Essentially, they are a form of mindfulness. The best kind of mindful hobby is one that is fun, repetitive, or engaging, requiring focus to complete effectively. They absorb our focus and mental energy, and we are incapable of worrying.

Many of us spend a lot of time on computers or other digital devices. We sit more now than we ever have in history. Physical movement and physical creation are needed. It is important these mindful activities are physical. You need to move or make something. These are restorative.

They are a balance to the cerebral activities that can tumble you into a worry state. When you are playing on your phone or tablet, you are still in your mind. While your thumbs may twitch, you are not really moving, not really creating.

Don't get me wrong! I love techno-gadgetry! I think they have interconnected the planet in a big way. They are important. And let's face it; they are here to stay. Balance is the important thing.

Spending time in mindful, physical activities are an important 'rest' from our usual activity.

I find a very beautiful peace when I am out running in nature; the flow of life, the swinging of my legs, the metronome of my heart, the rhythm, it soothes me. Now,

I know that running is not everyone's cup of tea! Fortunately, there is more than one type of tea!

You may already have an idea which hobby, craft, or sport gives you this absorbing, yet renewing quality. For some people, it might be dancing, singing, or colouring. For others, it might be flying an airplane or climbing a mountain. The activity itself is not as important as is the *mindful* nature of it.

Ask yourself: Are you able to worry while you do your mindful activity? Is it something you enjoy? Does it give you pleasure? When you are done your activity, how do you feel? Refreshed? Vital? Renewed?

If so, then that is the perfect choice for you.

Take a moment now to **book a time** in your calendar to spend time on your mindful activity. Booking it in your calendar means it will happen. Or, at least, it is more likely to happen than if you didn't. No excuses here. Make time for you!

Book it for as soon as you can, preferably, in the next week or two. Gift yourself the time to nourish and nurture yourself. Make space in your life for YOU!

Walking is the BEST Mindful Activity!

Now, that takes care of next week, but what about right now? Sometimes, our mindful activities take time, money, or resources we cannot access every day. But you *can* walk every day.

I like to pick activities that are zero excuse activities. Often we delay nurturing ourselves because we run into limited thinking. We falsely decide there is not enough time, money, availability or approval to take time to nurture our needs.

We decide that, if we don't have hours at hand, or piles of cash in the bank, or the blessing of those around us, we can't take care of ourselves. We often exacerbate this by choosing self-care activities that require a lot of time, money, or babysitting.

You *can* deeply nurture and nourish your inner self, with only a few short minutes, zero dollars, and you can pack up your kids and dogs and others and bring them along!

The easiest and most accessible mindful activity is walking.

Yup. Just going for a nature walk, even one minute, will shift everything.

And, you need not leave the city or your block to do it. Just go outside. We live on Planet Earth, so we are ALWAYS in nature!

Nature is inherently healing, calming, and mindful. Even if you have the perfect mindful activity picked out, I encourage you to take a nature walk at least once this week.

Not only is gentle exercise, like walking, loaded with health benefits, it is innately able to derail worry and reset our biology. It is rhythmic. It is centering. It is restful.

Now, if you cannot walk, roll! If you cannot roll, then seek out nature videos, nature sounds, or have a friend create a video of a nature walk they went on. You could even have them video call you in! Real-time nature walks!

Reset your Body-mind in Nature

The benefits of being in nature are profound. Every great master-teacher throughout our spiritual history sought inspiration, solace, and connection with the Divine in a nature retreat. God, it seems, lives in the natural world.

We become acutely aware of a larger consciousness at work below the hum of bees, or the slow growth of trees, or the soft wave of blades of grass, or the sweet songs and raucous calls of birds.

We live *in* nature.

Nature is all around us all of the time. Even in the most industrialized areas, there are still signs of nature if you look for them. There are birds, insects, plants, flowers, trees, fish, mammals, and (of course!) humans!

Humans are part of nature too! When you see another human being, you are looking at a part of nature itself.

Do not forget this. We are animals. Clever animals, but animals just the same.

So when you go on your mindful walk in nature, you need not *drive* anywhere! You can find nature right outside your front door.

The entire walk, look for life.

Look for nature.

Look for trees & birds & grass.

Notice the insects, the pets, the squirrels, the people.

Be aware of the whole of nature all around you in this moment.

Leave your phone behind. Leave your music player and headphones behind. Listen to the sounds and song that is already there.

Go by yourself or with others.

If you have small children or pets, let them bring you back to the mindful present moment, where they naturally live. Small people notice everything. Every bug and blade of grass and every different thing. It is all new to them. Allow their natural wonder to guide you to the present moment.

If you are walking with big people, older kids, and other adults, explain that this is a nature walk. You are looking for signs of nature the whole walk, and you won't be talking much.

Let **them** do whatever **they** choose to do. This is **your** walk, **your** practice. **They** don't have to join you in mindfulness for **you** to be mindful! If you catch yourself being annoyed by your traveling companions, just observe. They are helping you!

Return to the present moment with these questions:

'Where am I?'

'What am I doing?'

I am outside. I am walking. I am on the path. I am breathing. I am in nature. I am walking.

Go for as long as it is joyful. Return renewed.

Signs of Spring

Take a topic you worry about on a regular basis.

Now, spend 5 minutes writing a list of all the tiny ways that aspect of your life is improving. Reach towards hope and possibility.

Winter is over. Spring is coming. The ground is still frozen. How do you know spring is right around the corner?

Imagine springtime opening up and softening your worry.

Rest easy in the promise of new hope. Positive changes are occurring, just below the surface.

Spring is here! All around you. Have the courage to look.

Practice

It is said that the mind has no thought producing power, only thought pursuing power. In Vedic philosophy, the mind is not limited to just the body of the brain. The mind exists both within and outside the body. Thoughts, in this philosophy, originate outside of the body-mind. We do not produce or create thoughts; we only catch them as they travel through our mental fields. By this same line of reasoning, it is impossible to control thought, because it does not start from within us, but outside of us, just beyond our reach.

What we do have is the powerful ability to pursue our thoughts. We can choose which thoughts we follow. We can choose which thoughts are worthy of our time and attention. We have the powerful ability to focus on whatever we choose.

Worry can seem uncontrollable. We can get swept completely away by it and be pulled below by its mighty undertow. It can be powerful in its momentum, especially if it is a longstanding concern or is about something dear to us, like the safety and well-being of our children, our finances, our love lives, our health, and well-being.

When worry is strong, it can be a futile endeavor to struggle against it. The hardest worries to let go of are the ones that have a lot of emotional weight to them or are connected to an actual concern affecting you right now.

A huge trigger for worry in my world is anything connected to the safety and well-being of my son. If I even catch a whiff of anything that might be not okay with him, I can easily slip into worry, if not all out panic. It all ramps up very quickly. It is like a huge tidal wave catches me and tosses me way out to sea. I am no longer in control, yet worry feels like I am paddling back to shore.

The truth is, worry is much more like flailing in chaos than swimming. Worry is incapable of the methodical logic and planning needed to get anything productive accomplished. Worry can feel like a lot of effort is being made, but in the end all you end up with is sore arms and lungs full of water.

At its best, worry is a distraction, but it rarely accomplishes anything productive.

How to Let Go

A beautiful practice to deal with extreme worry and anxiety is simply to stop fighting it. Just allow your worry some space to exist. Acknowledge it. Give up the fight to suppress it. Anchor yourself in the idea that your worries maybe real. They could be completely valid.

So now what?

Remember to breathe.

Yes.

The worst **could** happen.

When a worry, especially a big one, is directly confronted, it often fizzles. There is nowhere left for it to go, but out.

All of the weight and force of it are dispersed, and all that remains is the tender thought that if the worst came true today, somehow, it will be all right.

You would find a way to pick up the pieces. You would mend what was broken and grieve what was lost. You would find a way to recover, as you have again and again, when other hardships have overcome you.

This practice is the equivalent of turning the ship to face the wave. Suddenly, you are slicing through it, riding it out, hanging on until the intensity drops and you can, once again, steer toward shore. To turn too soon toward joy when you are in the midst of a real concern or huge anxiety can pull you right under.

Instead, turn and face the problem head on. Acknowledge that you just don't know all the answers.

Feel the vulnerability. Stop suppressing it. That just makes it worse. Allow some room for faith to enter.

Faith is hope, unsupported by evidence.

Just get comfortable with being uncomfortable. Really feel it, without trying to numb it or run from it. Breathing is your best friend in this process. Breathing slowly and deeply and regularly will slow down your physiology and let the emotional wave pass through quickly.

Just for Today — Let Go Of The Struggle.

Just for today, acknowledge the worry you are feeling. Allow it to be. Acknowledge the grain of truth in it and accept the potential worst-case outcome.

How would you get through the worst case scenario if it was true? What are the resources you would call upon? How could you allow the Divine to support you in this? What if it was the Universe's problem to solve? How would you ask for help? Who would you ask for help?

Observe how it feels in your body when you give up the struggle, with even the smallest worry. Notice how your mind can shift towards solutions, rather than being fixated on the problem. Test this practice in your life as a powerful way to resolve worry in a shorter time than ever before.

Just for today... let go of the struggle with worry and embrace faith.

Intuition

I often get asked, how do you know if it is a false worry or fear, or if it is a real signal from your intuition, trying to protect you?

The very simple answer is you can only know by the way you feel. If you work with your intuition regularly, you will feel the difference between a clear 'no' response and a clear 'yes'. But, sometimes, fear can muddle up the signals.

The feeling of a clear 'no' is like running into a wall. There is resistance in your body, when you think of the 'no' option, but immediate relief when you think of the 'yes' option. When fear is active, the differences between a 'yes' and a 'no' is less clear, but you can still tell a slight difference, even if it is tiny.

One powerful way to get clarity is to give yourself some distance from the issue. We have all felt the value of hindsight, where looking back on a problem gives us clarity on where we went wrong or right.

Imagine you can give yourself that clarity, right now. Just by accessing the higher and wiser YOU, you can gain clarity on issues normally out of your reach.

Take a moment now to zoom out. Take a long look at your life. Get up high, away from the action. Think of it as the crane shot in a movie, the angle where you change the point of view from up close on the subject to high overhead, way up above.

Let me walk you through an example of how this 'zoom out' approach might work. Think about a time when you were procrastinating on an important task, say for work.

First, explore the tension of ease in your body when you think about delaying doing the task. Now, feel the tension when you think about working on it. Often, there is a tiny difference in how you feel about these two options, but you are too close to the problem to see it clearly.

Maybe you feel slightly worse when you think about delaying the work more. The fact there is a slight difference is a tiny indication of which direction you probably need to go. But really, at this point, all options feel awful, and the best course of action is to spend the time *now* to get clear, before you *choose* procrastinating or doing.

Zoom Out for Clarity

Imagine you can zoom out far enough you can see the whole of your life before you, the beginning and the end.

Zoom out even farther. Include the moments before you incarnated in this life and include the moments of reunification with the Divine after you have died.

From this expanded and aware place, where you can simply observe your life, which is the best choice?

Right away, the answer is supplied. "Just finish it!" The answer is clear. There is little emotional content in it; there is no disasterization, there is no hair-pulling terror. The answer is clear. The answer *feels* right. There is certainty in its character and voice, yet there is also a reassuring calmness. You can have a dialogue with this wisdom. You can ask questions and get clear answers. Those answers leave you feeling better, not worse.

More than anything, the voice of your deep wisdom, your intuitive voice, is clear, calm, and reassuring. This place within you believes in your abilities and will connect you to the resources you need.

Occasionally, your wise, intuitive, inner voice will choose option C, "none of the above" and will instead supply a creative alternative to your situation. You could get an answer like, "You need to talk to so-and-so" or "You need to read this resource first" or "You need to ask your boss for x, y, or z" or "*You* aren't supposed to be doing this at all. Delegate it to someone else."

Sometimes, procrastination, which is connected strongly to worry, is caused by a genuine need to slow down or stop in a certain area. Sometimes, you need more information before processing; sometimes, you are genuinely going in the wrong direction.

I find the more you follow your intuition, this confusion becomes rarer.

So take the zoom out approach! Let your wise inner voice speak and be reassured by its kind advice.

Affirmation Ladder

When you are in the grasp of worry, it can feel impossible to shift thoughts of hope, peace, and joy. Worry's innate nature is to use the power of fear to freeze and immobilize you. It is a protection mechanism gone awry.

Fear can protect us in a situation where we need to be still to avoid a predator's gaze. But being frozen in most other situations is unhelpful. Being and staying stuck creates more fear and worry. It is a self-perpetuating cycle, and it can sometimes seem like it is impossible to get out of a worried frame of mind when we are in it. There is so much momentum behind worried thoughts that trying to stop them is much like leaping in front of a speeding train. Not much good will come of it.

When you are in the middle of worry, the best course of action is to nudge it ever so slightly with an affirmation of faith, and the powerful momentum will carry that nudge along with it and do what worry does best, magnify it.

You get a slightly different stream of thought after using an affirmation, and your mind notices something is new in the habitual pattern.

By only adjusting the negative thought in a small way, the inner battle with the ego is never activated. The ego is unaware that any big thought shift is underway, and it is then safe to make a series of small adjustments in thought patterns that garner no inner resistance. The result is the ability to gradually shift your thoughts from worry to hope to faith.

Begin, as with the anger affirmations in the previous chapter, by ranking your current level of worry on a scale from zero to ten.

There is no judgment on whatever your current worry level is, so please be honest with yourself to get the most out of this exercise. No need to overthink it; just take the first answer that pops into your mind.

On a scale from 0 to 10, ten being completely frozen and consumed by fear, worry, and anxiety, so you cannot function, and zero being you feel wonderful, optimistic, and filled with faith.

Rate your current level of worry now. Based on your answer, practice the corresponding affirmation until it feels natural. Each affirmation is an acknowledgment and a little nudge. As you practice each one, for the level you are at, you will gradually work your way up, bit by bit, to faith, trust, and ease.

Practice each affirmation until it feels natural. Listen to the tension in your body. Stay with each affirmation. Linger. Let it really sink in until you no longer feel it is true for you, then go on to the next, lower numbered worry affirmation. Spend time with each one. Look in the mirror. Speak truth. Honour your body signals.

Letting Go of Worry Affirmation Ladder

0	Things always work out for me. I trust in Divine solutions.
1	I know I am always safe and loved. The Divine is on my side.
2	I believe in me. God/the Divine/the Universe does too.
3	My wise-self guides me to the best outcome. I listen to the voice of my soul.
4	I can see many possibilities. There are many options available to me now.
5	I am safe to grow and to change. I accept my human mistakes as a chance to grow and change. It is okay to be human!
6	I accept this situation for what it is. I allow life to be as it is.
7	Breathing in, I am here. Breathing out, it is now.
8	Even though I am really worried about this, I am willing to accept and love myself just as I am.
9	I am gripped with worry right now. It feels awful to be in this place, but I can take one tiny action right now to change. Just one tiny breath to let in freedom.
10	I am terrified and completely frozen by worry right now. Even though worry dominates my thoughts, I am still able to breathe. If I am still breathing, I still have a chance.

Using the Affirmation Ladder for Worry

Let me walk you through an example on how the Affirmation Ladder works for moving you from worry to faith.

So, let's say you are feeling really on edge lately. Maybe your thoughts keep coming back to the topic of money. Not having enough. Not earning enough. Extra expenses coming at you out of the blue. Try as you might to stay positive, you just keep getting stuck. You get right back on board the worry train — no stops.

This level of worry sounds like a 7 or 8.

Start with Worry Affirmation 8, "*Even though I am really worried about this, I am willing to accept and love myself just as I am.*"

Take a deep breath.

Now, does your body tighten or relax after repeating that affirmation? If you tighten up, that means you need to try out Worry Affirmation 9, "*I am gripped with worry right now. It feels awful to be in this place, but I can take one tiny action right now to change. Just one tiny breath to let in freedom.*"

If Worry Affirmation 8 makes you feel some relief, then you are right on the money (pun intended)! Keep repeating number 8 for the day. See if your worry eases. It is totally okay if this takes some time.

Sometimes you will feel like an affirmation, though good, doesn't quite fit. In this case, try out the next one up the ladder, number 7, "*Breathing in, I am here. Breathing out, it is now.*"

Keep tuning in and rating your worry level every so often and watch as your levels climb all the way up to "*Things always work out for me. I trust in Divine solutions.*"

Faith as an Antidote to Worry

Faith. It can be a loaded word for some. In its most negative connotation, faith is associated with blindness, with disregard for new information, new facts, or reality.

It is understandable that people might shy away from the word faith, especially if they have been exposed to fundamentalism in any form. But I want to redefine faith here. Faith is so effective at resolving worry. I really want to wash away the negative from this beautiful word and restore it to its best and most helpful definition.

Faith is trust. Faith is belief that things will somehow work out, even when there is nothing in front of you to show you it will. Faith is belief in the mystery; there are forces at work in the universe that are far greater and wiser than any of us. Mystery. We don't know. We may never know. And yet, we trust.

Every time you get out of bed, you are putting faith in something. There is ground below your feet; there is a sun in the sky; there is air enough to breathe. Somehow. No matter how bad things get, you will get through.

Faith requires us to dance with our vulnerability. When we feel most vulnerable, worry pops right up. Right in our face. Instead of fighting it, faith offers us a tool to hand over our worries to something greater.

There is a deep intelligence and wisdom in the Universe. It operates at the frequency of love. Love is an organizing force. Love creates miracles. Those miracles come within reach when we recognize the protective and loving Universe is working for us, behind the scenes.

The love the Universe has for you is powerful. Every experience is an opportunity to open to this love in a deeper way. It is all for you. Open up and let that love and support flow in.

Recognize how you are helped. Look for little signs, those Signs of Spring. They just pop up everywhere when you look for them. They are fed by your faith.

Your faith that things will get better, that you are strong enough to get through, that you can access all the support you need, that things are already going well, that as you read this, you are receiving support you will experience very soon.

Faith stops worry. It is not based on false facts. It is based on the reality that is all around you, right now, that you have millions of blessings right in front of your eyes.

Take a few moments now. List a few of your millions of blessings. List your strengths. List your resources.

CHAPTER SIX:

Gratitude

'Thank you' is the best prayer that anyone could say. I say that one a lot. Thank you expresses extreme gratitude, humility, understanding.

~ Alice Walker

Gratitude is a powerful force for change in our lives. There is no wonder why it is the third Reiki Ideal. Gratitude is pure magic. Turning your thoughts toward all your many blessings will expand them. More importantly, you receive the immediate benefit of an improved mood.

Even if you had difficulty releasing anger and worry throughout the exercises in previous chapters, you will see an immediate benefit from a practice of gratitude and appreciation. For one thing, gratitude immediately gets you out of the role of victim. Even in the darkest of days, there is always something to be grateful for.

If you can practice gratitude deliberately and on a daily basis, you will find positive emotions and spontaneous gratitude just popping up as your first response in any situation, "good" or "bad."

Gratitude is a Feeling

Appreciation* is, perhaps, a cleaner way of expressing gratitude, as it makes you focus on the positive qualities of the object of your gratitude.

Often, as children, gratitude was extorted from us by our well-meaning parents and teachers. We were commanded to say 'thank you' whether or not we felt grateful. Being grateful can quickly become a social obligation, rather than a deeply felt appreciation. Ultimately, it is not the words that matter the most, but the feeling behind them.

The feeling you are looking for is a softness in your heart, an openness, a generosity, a good feeling. You naturally want to give to others when you feel gratitude and appreciation.

Smiles come easily to your face, and your outlook on life is uplifted. You are able to easily notice the kindness and generosity in those around you. You notice people being kind to you and to others. You get many reminders of how abundant, healthy, and happy you really are. You are able to easily see these things appearing in your current experience when you focus on gratitude.

Gratitude is naturally attractive. A feeling of gratitude creates and releases a powerful energy. That natural energetic force is a match to the energy of the Universe, the universal life

---

* Appreciation is another way of thinking about gratitude. Abraham (from the work of Esther Hicks) cautions the use of the word 'gratitude' in their works about the Law of Attraction, as gratitude can be tinged with obligation and angst.

Ultimately, it is how you relate to the words of gratitude or appreciation that should dictate which one will work best for you. For me, I tend to use the words interchangeably. I really like the word gratitude, so I use it every day. Please substitute the word 'gratitude' with the word 'appreciation' as you read this chapter if appreciation has more ease and less resistance for you.

force energy flowing all around us. When you are grateful, you have the ear of God. The Divine resonates at the frequency of love and gratitude, so when you feel that way, you are connected powerfully to that wonderful Source energy.

When you focus, even briefly, on something you are grateful for, you create a ripple in the energy field of the Universe. Now, you are speaking in a way the Universe can hear. Anything you are truly and honestly grateful for will grow and magnify. You will get more of it; you will get better and better quality results. You will see evidence and synchronicities all around you. Your deepest desires are within reach when you reach for gratitude.

It is very important to *feel* gratitude. Remove 'should' from the picture and your vocabulary. When it comes to gratitude and appreciation, there is no need to force yourself to muster gratitude for something or something if you do not feel it. If you are not genuinely *feeling* grateful, then skip that state-ment. In time, your feelings of gratitude will naturally expand to include your challenges as well as your successes, but for now, just know that even a tiny bit of genuine gratitude will do the job.

There is no need to manufacture gratitude for things or events you do not *feel* gratitude for, but you do need to honestly look around your experience and find something, anything, you genuinely appreciate. It could be something *small*, like the fact that you are breathing, or that you are able to read this sentence. Or it could be something *profound*, like the fact that you are breathing and able to read this sentence.

It is perfectly okay if you are having trouble finding any-thing in your experience to be grateful for. You are still a good person!

Gratitude is a skill.

It must be practiced. It is an art form.

Gratitude Creates Grateful Relationships

Often our family, friends, and culture encourage complaining and criticism. Sometimes, complaining about our lives is a point of connection with others. If we start being grateful, getting happier, and genuinely appreciating the beauty in the world, we can find a natural distance occurring within our relationships that are based on wingeing, whining, pity, and complaining.

The shift in these relationships can be scary, especially if they are your primary relationships or with people you really love and care about. Know that, while your relationships may shift and change, the ones based on love will stay in your life. The outer dynamic may change, but ultimately, as you improve your life and become happier, the people who genuinely love and care for you will accommodate the new person you are.

Some people and relationships may shift completely out of your life too.

I want to assure you this change is absolutely to your benefit. When you shift the internal landscape, everything on the surface changes too. When those shifts are ones of happiness and lasting contentment, then the outer changes in your life, regardless of how it may seem at first, are exactly what is needed.

You are making room in your life for relationships of the heart, based on love, optimism, and support. Those relationships based on complaining, negativity, and co-dependence will naturally fade away or change. Sometimes, the change is the person leaving; sometimes, the change is the person completely changing how they interact with you.

As if by magic, as you begin to be nicer to yourself, others begin to be nicer to you. The more you appreciate, the more there is to be appreciated.

This is a zero effort model of change! Aside from the tiny effort to think a grateful thought, you need not do anything else to get 'others' to stop complaining or gossiping. All those critical ones in your outer life are only there because there is an internal process within you that is still generating critical thoughts and energy.

Once the gratitude thoughts and feelings become dominant in your body-mind, the outer world changes, yes, but your reactions to it are also transformed.

The Power of Our Stories and the Book That Changed My Life

I experienced this shift in friendships with the very first book I read on personal development. A friend I had for years completely dropped out of my life when I began reading *Women Who Run with the Wolves* by Clarissa Pinkola Estés.

In the book, the details and construction of fairy tales were decoded. The ancient wisdom contained within these stories shed light on the power of how a personal story is told can completely transform a person from the inside out. I was absorbed by its pages.

The transformative power of these fairy tales, written at time when the magic and mystery of women and their power as guardians of the Life-Death-Life cycle, that *power* within, that completely changed how I saw myself and encouraged me to start telling a different story about my life.

As I changed the story I was telling about myself, I began to change. It was the first time in my life where I could just turn out the bedside light and fall right asleep. Up till then, I was gripped with waves of worry for an hour before I would finally fall into exhausted sleep. Before reading the book, I would wake up in much the same state as I fell asleep, gripped with worry and terror. I would worry about failing, making mistakes, what other people thought of me, what might happen tomorrow, endlessly ruminating over the events of the day.

After reading the first chapter of *Women Who Run with the Wolves*, I started to not only fall asleep effortlessly, but I also started to wake up full of optimism and positivity.

I started to look for all of the reasons that my life was great. I looked for the possibilities. I saw the potential for things to get better, instead of worse. For the first time in my life, the fear of the future and terror of the 'mistakes' of the past did not haunt me. I was free. I was changing. I was becoming unbearably happy.

You can imagine how obnoxious I was to my friend. After years of being a habitual worrier and complainer, I changed overnight to a positive, ridiculously happy person, full of advice and commentary about how she could get happy too.

Yeah.

When Louise Hay says "Don't fix your friends", that is very sage advice. However, I would not encounter *You Can Heal Your Life* for several years after this.

My friend also changed almost overnight as I did. She just stopped talking to me. Completely. Even if we were in the same room, and I was talking directly to her. No response. It was the closest I have ever felt to being completely invisible. It was downright spooky.

Our friendship was over, and it was all because I changed. I refused to go back to who I was, and she couldn't stand the new effusive and helpful me.

I was faced with a choice. I chose to be happy and explore this new 'me'. The old friendship just couldn't survive the abrupt transition.

Being miserable with company is still being miserable.

I chose being happy and alone.

In reality, I wasn't alone long. By continuing to cultivate happiness and telling a better story about myself, I found new friends, deep and lasting friends, who were as interested in growth, happiness, and change as I am. And they have continually been entering my life ever since. The more I am 'me', the *real* me, the more I find similar people, who are fun to hang out and have tea with.

Where there is a void, nature will fill it.

Do not fear the *voids* in your life. They are just the wilderness times, when magic is under every leaf and twig.

Chance and random encounters occur the most when we are in the void wildlands. The potential for radical and permanent and positive change is the highest when we let go of what we knew and embrace the tender new story and green sprigs of happiness taking root in our hearts.

Be grateful for this moment of magic you are in, right now, as you read these words. You are already changed. You are.

Meditation

No matter where you are on your gratitude journey, meditation on gratitude will bring immediate benefits. Whether you are new to the concept of gratitude or you are experienced as an appreciator, you will receive tremendous benefit from the following meditation.

The purpose of this meditation is to get into the same feeling and energy of gratitude. When you are *feeling* gratitude, you are vibrating at the same frequency as the Universe. And the Universe is supremely grateful for YOU!

Gratitude Meditation

Start by sitting up straight. Take a very deep breath.

Let it all the way out.

Take another deep breath, and let it, gently, out.

Once more, breathe in and all the way out.

Very Good.

Now bring your awareness to the tip of your nose. Just gently focus on this part of your body.

Breathe easily.

Breathe gently.

As you focus on the tip of your nose, become aware of the purpose of this part of your body.

Feel the air, softly flowing around it as you breathe gently.

Easy and relaxed, your nose and its precious tip are an important part of your biology.

The tip of your nose is an important part of your identity.

Large or small, your nose rests easily on the center of your face.

Your nose makes you recognizable to others. The tip of your nose is a precious place, a meeting point of the outer world and your inner world.

It is the point where 'they' stop and 'you' begin.

This is an important place on your body, where you can begin to redefine what it means to be YOU.

This is the place where you decide what is right for you or wrong for you. This is the place where you are able to distinguish where you choose to be and how you choose to behave.

This is a very important part of your body.

Spend a few moments now, thanking your nose tip for its valuable service and contribution to your life.

Thank you, nose tip, for being part of my experience!

Feel your gratitude and appreciation reflected back to you as your nose tip thanks you for your unique expression in this physical life.

Now, bring your awareness to your bones. Think about the 206 bones that are part of your skeleton.

Recognize the contribution your bones make to your life.

Feel the solidity of your bones.

Recognize their ability to flow and shift, depending on the demands of your life.

Your bones are strong and provide shape and support to your physical body. And they are also dynamic living tissues that house your bone marrow, the source of your immune cells.

Bones protect what is most precious, your heart, your lungs, your brain. And they also protect each and every cell in your wonderful body.

Your bones support you, without question. Through all of the decisions and experiences of your life, your bones are always there for you, lending their structure and wisdom to every step and every choice you make.

Spend a few moments in deep reverence to the wisdom that lives in your bones. Honour that part of you that honours YOU.

Thank you bones, for your wisdom. Thank you for always being there.

Feel your gratitude and appreciation reflected back to you as your bones thank you for your wise presence and graceful support in this physical life.

Now, turn your attention to the strongest muscle in your body, your heart.

For as long as you have lived, as long as you live, your heart beats.

Become aware of this powerful and steady part of your body.

Notice your heart's gentle beat, now.

Just gently observe its rhythm.

Notice its gentle wave, pulsing right in the centre of your chest.

Notice its devotion to you.

Notice your heart's natural ability to respond with ease to whatever experience your life has offered you.

Your heart can keep pace with you as you run and jump and swim and sprint.

Your heart can alert you to love as it skips merrily when you meet your partner.

Your heart lets you know when you have found safety and support, with softness and ease.

Your heart glows with courage and compassion with its every devoted beat.

If you listen, gently, to your heart now, it will offer you the perfect advice on how to live a joyful and free life. Listen now.

Spend a few moments thanking your heart for all its love, courage, and strength.

Thank you, heart, for each and every beat.

Feel your gratitude and appreciation reflected back to you as your heart thanks you for your courageous journey in this physical life.

Rest here for a moment.

Bask in the joy of it all.

Take a deep breath.

Say thank you.

Wiggle your fingers and your toes in gratitude.

Give yourself a hug and a stretch. Your meditation is done.

Sharing Circle

Spend the next 5 minutes writing about your experience in the meditation.

Did the meditation change the affection you feel for your body?

What other, overlooked things in your life do you feel grateful for?

Write a fast list of every tiny thing that you feel grateful for.

Self Care & Love

A gratitude practice is the epitome of self-care. When we are grateful, we are actually making an unspoken statement to the Universe that we are worthy of the good we have in our lives. Gratitude is such a powerful force that we are even sending out the signal that we are worthy of *far more* than we can even imagine.

Sometimes we have been conditioned to believe we are inherently **un**worthy of our good, or that we must **do** something in order to deserve it.

The flawed premise we so often hold is that we must earn our good, and that God is withholding his love and grace from us, until we meet a set of stringent rules and do the proper amount of penance for our unworthiness.

This belief will not only block our ability to manifest the lives we choose and most definitely deserve and are worthy of, but it also blinds us to all of the good we already have in our lives. For, if we acknowledge that we are surrounded by blessings, but yet we feel inherently unworthy of them, we are unable to see what is right in front of us. We are **surrounded** by good.

Gratitude and self-worth are inextricably linked. We must believe in our worth in order to fully recognize the thousands of ways we are already blessed. We are blessed.

Reading is a Blessing

If you can read this book, you have already won the birth lottery. You were born or were raised in a family or culture that valued literacy. You were able, at some point in your life, likely when you were very young, to go to school and have teachers and parents teach you to read.

This is a huge feat. So many millions of people are not so lucky. They never learned to read and so are unable to teach their children to read. They are also likely living in poverty and are unable to send their children to school.

The gift of literacy is not to be understated or dismissed. Being able to read gives you huge advantages in life. Reading opens doors to knowledge that might otherwise be closed. If you have an internet connection at home or access to one at your public library, you are doubly or triply lucky. With the vast resources available today, just a search term away, you are able, as never before in history, to improve your life merely through the ability to read. Your ability to read and willingness to learn can completely change your life.

You have huge resources available to you, and you are probably already a super smart duckie!

With everything you have learned in your life, you have resources that can improve your current state, without spending an extra cent. Reading is powerful. Reading is a gift you were given. It is yours, and you have it forever.

You are worthy of your ability to read.

Not only that, you likely see reading as a right. Indeed, literacy is a human right. You are entitled to your ability to read, simply because you are human. Reading is a basic skill that enhances your well-being, and you did not need to *earn* it.

Extend that same feeling you have towards your literacy to all the other aspects of your life. Anything you want or desire — you're as worthy of that as you are your ability to read. All of the millions of blessings you already have are the same as your ability to read. You have them, and literacy, because you *ARE*. You need not do anything else. You are enough.

Just as you did not have to earn your right to read, you also do not need to earn or justify any other blessing or desire you may have. Consider a blessing you already have, but perhaps you downplay or hide it altogether. When we minimize our blessings to ease the discomfort of others, we are secretly undermining our path to happiness. We send a signal to our subconscious minds that we do not truly appreciate or feel like we are deserving of our blessing. We may have been taught that it is more important to keep everyone else comfortable than to be ourselves or enjoy our good fortune. To be 'nice', under this false idea, we must not be our bright and shiny selves, because people living in the ego would feel uncomfortable. The result is that, over time, the blessing disappears.

The universe and your subconscious mind will work towards giving you a state of comfort. If you feel uncomfortable with your current level of happiness, then you will subconsciously find ways to undermine it. This is the inner saboteur at work!

When we feel uncomfortable with our success or good fortune, we will always end up with less success. It is really the Universe's way of giving you ease. If you feel uncomfortable with all your blessings, the last thing a kind and loving Universe will give you is more things to feel uncomfortable about.

Even if you *say* you want more blessings in your life, the Universe is listening to the way you *feel*. You can only receive what you are capable of feeling *comfortable* with, so let's increase your comfort level!!

Just for Today — Feel your Worthiness

Just for today, acknowledge that you are as worthy of all blessings in your life, and the ones you wish for, as you are of your ability to read.

Take a blessing in your life that is the greatest. Pick just one thing, event, experience, or relationship you value above all else.

This is your number one blessing.

Think about your number one blessing. Feel the sensations in your body, heart, and skin when you tune deeply into this blessing. Remember what it was like when it first arrived in your experience. Feel this deeply, now.

Now, think about your ability to read. Feel how innately deserving of this blessing of literacy you are. Feel how you were worthy of the skill of reading, even before you were born. Immerse yourself in the experience of that deep and matter of fact worthiness.

Now, feel the truth of this: You are as worthy of your greatest blessing as you are of your ability to read.

You need not do anything other than exist to be worthy of your number one blessing.

You are completely worthy of this blessing.

You are completely worthy of your literacy.

Your blessing and your literacy are equal. Both are yours. Both are yours, because you are YOU. They are freely claimed by you as yours. You are entitled to all this and more.

Now turn your thoughts to your greatest wish. The experience, event, object, or relationship you truly and deeply desire.

Bring to mind your deep longing for this new, and on its way, blessing.

This blessing is just beyond your vision at this point. When it arrives, it will greatly exceed your expectations and will be far, far greater than you could ever imagine.

This great blessing that is on its way to you now is the same as your ability to read.

Your literacy and your new blessing are the same.

You deserve both, simply because you exist.

They are yours.

One is present and part of your everyday blessings; the other is on its way to becoming part of your everyday blessings. Both are yours. You are worthy of both, because you are human.

Spend a few minutes allowing the deep feeling of worthiness to flow in equal measure to all your blessings, present, past, and future. Let your worthiness of literacy be your guide. Seek to achieve the same feeling in your heart and body when you think of your worthiness of your blessings and your worthiness of your literacy. They are the same.

Just for today... know you are worthy of all this and more.

Signs of Spring

Gratitude creates more gratitude.

Notice all of the ways your life is changing. Good or bad, every event can bring gratitude. Even events we perceive as negative, truly are blessings in disguise.

These 'negative' moments teach us where we need to grow, rethink, retrace, regroup.

Sometimes, being sent 'back to the drawing board' is a necessary step in our expansion.

If we truly want to grow in our lives, we must mine our failures and tragedies for the gifts they hold. The only true failure is to think there is nothing to learn from failure.

List 5 Signs of Spring within an area of your life you perceive to be a failure. Notice the good, green, new shoots of life, even within destruction. Notice how a tiny bit of gratitude can transform even this painful experience to one of growth.

Intuition

The inner saboteur is at work any time we have trouble accessing our gratitude. The urge to push away or diminish our good is actually a misguided self-protection measure. It is meant as an attempt to insulate us from vulnerability.

If we deny or are unaware of all of our blessings, then they cannot be taken away. The pain of losing something that gives us joy is terrible. We have a self-preservation instinct that seeks to keep us safe at all costs, even if the cost is our ability to experience the very life we are seeking.

There can be this twin push and pull occurring within us. On one hand, we want our lives to be brilliant, shining, fulfilling, successful, and joyous; yet, on the other hand, we are desperate to minimize our pain and exposure.

We choose safety over joy.

Or, really, we *think* we do.

It is not real safety that the inner saboteur seeks. It is actually a dull void, a dusty, empty place, where change is impossible, and no one ever gets hurt, ever.

REAL safety is only found in the certainty that life is inherently unpredictable, but you will always recover and find a way through whatever hardships you might have. Being resilient and knowing you have resources to call upon — friends, family, community, inner strength, and wisdom — this is what true safety and security is based on.

The inner saboteur goes to work especially hard, when we have the most to be thankful for. Unless we have directly confronted and dealt with our tendency to keep ourselves small, the inner saboteur probably is still at work, undermining our success.

There is one sure way to know if this an issue for you. Think about the major areas of your life: family, relationships, finances, work, friendships, spirituality, and health. Within the past year, have you had crisis after crisis in one or more areas? How often are you needing to regroup and start again? Are there areas of your life where you seem to try and fail, try and fail, and try and fail in a seemingly endless loop?

If so, chances are high that having success in these areas of life are highly correlated with failure, setbacks, and delays. This is often associated with feelings of being uncomfortable with success or needing to fit in and be approved of by a group of people who are uncomfortable with your successes.

We can become blind to our inner saboteur, because it is gifted in the art of deception. The true art of sabotage is to make it seem like our successes were all an accident or that our failures were because it was all broken in the first place. Blame is shifted to others, and we walk away from the smoking wreckage of our lives, shrugging our shoulders and shaking our heads.

The inner saboteur's job is to make it someone else's fault and in so doing makes us perpetually its victim. For when we are not responsible for our lives, we are also not powerful. We get tricked into thinking things are impossible or that we are weak and incapable. This is simply not true. We always have the power of transformation and transcendence within us. In fact, it is only a moment, a thought, away.

Gratitude immediately diminishes the power of the inner saboteur. It cannot openly contradict something as uplifting as gratitude, lest it be lured out of the shadows and seen for what it is.

Gratitude and appreciation for *all* life circumstances requires us to leave the role of victim. We start looking at all of our tragedies in a new light. Gratitude for the tough times prompts us to consider this: Maybe, life is not happening *to* us; maybe life is happening *for* us. Maybe, we are the architects of our own lives, and we are creating it all. Maybe we can find a benefit from each and every experience we have ever had.

When we are in a state of gratitude, we are in the flow of LIFE. We are aligned with our Source of abundance, divinity, and health in all forms. Source is always, ALWAYS, able to see the positive in every experience. From that broad and expanded view, the beauty of our soul path is abundantly clear. All of the pieces are within view, and we can see we have a far greater benefit from our struggles than detriment.

This Divine-eye view can see each failure creates expansion, growth, and clarity. From this wise angle, we can see each event as the gift it truly is. They are all blessings.

When we develop the skill of focus, to see from the Divine-eye view, we see our failures as hidden gifts; we access a deep power to transform and change. We no longer fear failure, and so we are freed from it. We no longer fear success, and so it is ours. We release the need to diminish ourselves, because we can access the truth: We are all divine, glorious beings, who are truly worthy of all the GOOD the universe has to offer and then some.

If we can rejoice in every experience, we are assured a beautiful and prosperous life. It is all happening perfectly and at the perfect time.

The moment you choose a thought of gratitude, you stop resisting the tremendous abundance, health, good fortune, and love on its way to you RIGHT now. It is only a thought away.

Understanding the Intuition in your Body

Gratitude immediately stops negative thinking and can quickly change the vibrational signal you are sending to the Universe. Gratitude puts you in alignment with the Divine, and that alignment makes it easier to accurately hear your intuitive messages.

Your intuition can warn you when you are self-sabotaging. When you are conscious of your self-sabotage, then you can take deliberate steps to stop and get back into alignment. If you are unaware of when you are blocking your own good, a gratitude practice can bring that to light.

Notice when you are resisting gratitude in your life. Where are you blocked? What parts of your life are continually failing? Sometimes you need to do a bit of detective work to figure out what is going on. Your sabotage acts could happen either within the area giving you problems or within the area that is your strongest.

When life starts to get really good for you, does something 'bad' happen to bring you down? Do you fight with your spouse? Do you gain weight? Do you lose your job? Do your friends abandon you?

Begin to look at these 'bad' events as an external result of an *internal* vibration. All of those things could only occur if you were a vibrational match to them. That is **your** work, to shift the internal vibration, so you get the results you are wanting.

I find that your physical body can be one of your greatest tools in discovering your hidden resistance.

Mona Lisa Schultz, a medical intuitive and author, often says that, if you ignore your intuition, it goes into your body in the form of illness. These illnesses are **not** random, though. They are directly related to the nature of the hidden issue. Your body-mind cannot suppress intuition for long, without creating havoc within your system.

The hidden information can be brought to light. You can decode your illnesses and learn what is just beyond your conscious mind. Your aches, pains, accidents, illnesses, bumps, and bruises are all information you can decode. You can gain a greater understanding of what your intuition is trying to tell you. Once you get the message, the need for the illness disappears.

Of course, it is best to learn to interpret your intuition directly, before it manifests as illness. As you become more and more connected to your body-mind and your intuition, you will be able to shift the energy before any negative effects occur.

Your Body as an Intuition Receiver

Your intuition has a lot to say about the aspect of your life that needs attention. Sometimes your intuition gets your attention by speaking through your body. Gratitude for your body and its signals helps to ease any discomfort you might experience in your body. By writing out what is happening in your body and doing a little decoding work, we get a deeper appreciation for just how much wisdom the body-mind actually has. These physical conditions we experience are not random at all. We have all the wisdom and intuition we will ever need, living right within us all the time.

The beautiful thing is, as we expand and develop our intuition, our emotional state and physical health improve. We no longer need these hidden messages, because we are listening to them every single day. We no longer suppress or deny our intuition, once we understand that it can never really be silenced; it just gets louder and more clear by communicating through the body

Your body is a guide to get clear. If you feel congestion, restriction, or pain in a part of your body, that body part is linked to an area of your life, where you may also be suppressing your intuition. You can unlock both the mystery of the body and your intuition with this process. Even things going wrong within the body can hold a huge blessing when you explore the meaning behind them.

Here is the decoding tool that may help you understand your personal body-mind intuition.

1. Scan your body for any condition affecting your experience right now. Pick one area that gives you the most trouble.

2. Spend the next few minutes writing down what this body part does.

   • Write down the purpose within your physical body.

   • Write about how it works.

   • What is it connected to in the rest of your body?

   • Use your own language, just write about what this body part does in general, right off the top of your head.

3. Decode the description with the Body-Mind Intuition Decoder table below. Replace the body part word with the life area word or words from the table.

4. Now try writing about how your body is misbehaving. Describe the condition, what makes it worse, what makes it better, how you cope with the symptoms, and how you feel when it is better.

5. The last step in this exercise is to express true gratitude for the 'negative' physical condition as a Divine messenger.

These body messages are no longer required for your intuition to gain your attention. It is a final step in healing to acknowledge the benefits you gained by having this experience. The wisdom, lessons, and compassion for yourself and others that occur when you experience a physical ailment is something that can serve you and your growth very well. Being grateful for an outwardly negative experience will not create a repeat of it, but rather, it will actually erase the need to experience it again.

You can basically thank your illness, express gratitude for all you have learned, and now that you have learned your lessons and adopted a new pattern, the need for the illness is no longer there. Once we fully release the need for the illness, we stop experiencing it.

Each body part is connected to a different aspect of our lives. If we replace the body part names with a keyword for the life area it is connected to, we get a different picture of our health and also how it relates to the broader context of our lives. Take the list below and substitute the life area keyword for each body part.

Body-Mind Intuition Decoder

Body Part	Life Area
Head	Thoughts, Determination, Choices
Face	Relationships, Being Seen, Acknowledgement
Brain	Process, Intuition, Memory
Nerves	Communication, Unlimited energy
Eyes/Sight	Understanding, Curiosity
Ears/Hearing	Individuality, Awareness
Nose/Smell	Identity, Direction
Neck	Life Path, Ideas, Individuality, Justice

Body Part	Life Area
Spine	Life, Energy flow, Integrated relationships,
Back	Support, Preparedness,
Lower Back	Work, Money
Mid Back	Self Worth, Gratitude
Upper Back	Order, Control, Social Responsibility
Shoulders	Responsibility, Attitude, Parenthood
Elbows	Rest, Simplicity
Wrists	Practicality
Hands	Capability
Fingers	Details
Kidneys	Clarity, Freedom, Independence
Bladder	Patience, Support network,
Stomach	Power, Transformation, Growth
Small Intestine	Inner child, Playfulness
Large Intestine	Flow, Ease, Non-attachment, Independence, Stability
Liver	Emotional Filter, Happiness, Contentment
Gall Bladder	Decisions, Kindness, Responsibility for self
Pancreas	Happiness, Dynamic transformation, wealth
Connective tissue	Connections, Dependence, Network between self and the world and the divine.
Spinal Cord	Energy Flow
Spinal Discs	Interdependencies, Support, Protecting communication
Lower Body	Support Network
Upper Body	Spiritual Support
Left side	Mother, feminine, receptivity, allowing, Being a Girl/Woman
Chest	Self-Expression, Bravery, Kindness
Ribs	Protection, Defending the vulnerable, Courage
Arms	Strength, Deliberate Action
Bones	Family, Courage, Stillness, Determination
Joints	Change, Flexibility
Muscles	Action, Passion, Strength, Work
Metabolism	Interdependence, Connections,
Uterus	Creativity, Wealth, Strength, Divine Timing, Patience with Life Processes

Body Part	Life Area
Vagina/Vulva	Beginnings, Sexuality, Spiritual Doorway
Ovaries	Creative potential, Adulthood, Responsibility
Breasts	Nurturing, Heartfulness
Penis	Impermanence, New Ideas, Sexuality
Prostate	Switching focus, Trust in Divine Path
Testicles	Creative potential, Adulthood, Responsibility
Spleen	Peacefulness, Safety, Secrets, Open and Honest communication
Hormones	Communication, Trust, Balance, Inner Guidance
Heart	Love, Courage, Joy
Arteries and Veins	Communication, Steady Abundance, Allowing Flow
Lungs	Self-Expression, Freedom, Room for your Inner Work in your Outer life
Throat	Honesty, Truth, Justice
Sinuses	Inner knowing, Hope, Honesty
Teeth	Decisions, Longevity
Jaw	Public speaking, Honesty, Fairness
Tongue	Joyful sampling of life, Freedom to choose, Individuality.
Skin/Touch	Intuition, Space, Joyful silence, Meditation, Pleasure
Legs	Stability, Flexibility, Movement
Knees	Honour, Commitment, Follow-through, Momentum
Ankles	Balance, Pleasure
Feet	Life Path, Sacred self, Buddha-nature, Seeking Divinity within, Following, Leading
Toes	Direction, Control, Balance, Moving
Hips	Purpose, Balance
Right side	Father, masculine, Activity, action, Being a Boy/Man

Note: If you take meditation or need medical procedures to alleviate your condition, you can use the word 'help' when you are rewriting.

If you are taking a lot of medication, ask yourself if you need help in other areas of your life, but you have a difficult time asking for it. Have you equated needing help with being weak?

If so, I invite you to release all shame connected to helping and being helped.

The easiest way to reform your opinion of help is to remember what it was like being a newborn baby. You needed help for **everything**, even moving your head. There was no shame placed on you then, when you honestly couldn't do it for yourself, because everyone, including you, had the wisdom that you were exactly where you needed to be. You are not more or less worthy of love because you can do so many things now that you couldn't when you were a baby.

Doing more does not earn you more love. The Universe, like a good parent, loves you completely and totally. The Universe does not withhold love, because you need help sometimes; it is only grateful that you made your needs known.

You need to ask for help and know it is part of the condition of being human. And there is zero shame in being human. Being human, needing help, giving help, working together with our restrictions, this is a great gift.

Our challenges and limitations inspire massive creativity and solutions. Our willingness to help and be helped is what adds delight and grace to our human experience.

Giving feels **so** incredibly good.

Just know that, when you ask for help when you need it (including lifesaving medical treatments and medication), you are allowing someone else to fulfill their Dharma, their life purpose, as helper and healer. You are also expanding your experience and receiving help and having the wisdom to cry out when you need to; it is part of our hard-wiring for survival.

Here is an example of how to get the most from this writing process. At the time of writing this, my lower back was giving me some trouble. So, using my lower back as an example:

The lower back is a support structure, as part of my lower spine. It flexes and flows with my hips as I walk, move, and bend. It is both strong and flexible, as it is made of bone, connective tissue, nerves, discs, and muscles. My lower back and spine protect my spinal cord and the nerves that reach my lower body. All of the messages from and commands to my lower body travel through my lower spinal column. My lower back allows me to walk, jump, sit, stand, and do all of my daily activities. My lower back works by having a balance between support and flexibility. My bones are strong to protect my spine. My discs are tough, yet somewhat flexible to allow movement, within reason. My muscles are attached to my limbs and core abdominals and to the rest of my spine to allow movement. My muscles push and pull my limbs and legs around, because they are connected to the strength and support of my spine. All of these pieces work together and support each other to create movement, communication, and stability.

When I use the Body-Mind Intuition Decoder for my earlier description I get this:

My work is a support structure of my life. It flexes and flows with purpose when I travel through my life. It is both strong and flexible, as it is made of family connections, communication, interdependencies, and action. My work and life protect my energy flow and the communication that reaches my support network. All of the messages to and commands from my support network travel through my energy flow. My work allows me to do all of my daily activities. My work works by having a balance between support and flexibility. My family is strong to protect my life. My interdependencies are tough, yet somewhat flexible, to allow movement, within reason. My actions push and pull my movements and stability around, because they are connected to the strength and support of my life. All of these pieces work together and support each other to create movement, communication, and stability.

Sometimes, you might need to shift the sentences a bit to make it read better, but you get the idea.

For me, when I addressed the need to shift my work situation, my back got better too. Of course, I did all the physical therapies that I needed to restore strength and flexibility to my spine (Yay yoga!), but I knew that, until I changed my work-family-life balance, I would have the same old repeated pattern of my back randomly giving out on me.

By acknowledging the deeper pattern and the interconnected nature of our outer lives with our body, we can begin to make deliberate changes in our lives that support not only our mental and emotional well-being, but also our physical health.

This exploration directly addresses our inner saboteur by understanding the cause of physical distress in a very specific way. We gain insight into our inner nature. We are given freedom from self-destructive patterns and thoughts.

For example, if you get a cold every time you overbook your schedule, but you do not give yourself permission to rest, unless you are really sick, then you will continue in this overwork-illness cycle until you finally acknowledge that it is okay to **take time off** and say **no** when we are **well**.

The new pattern is resting when you need to. Until you begin to meet that need when you are healthy, the need for illness will be ever-present. Getting just a **bit** sick serves a purpose in an odd way when you have not learned the needed practice of saying no or setting boundaries. This may or may not be the case for you, so do the writing exercise and tune in to see what may be the underlying cause for you.

The really cool thing is that, as soon as the new pattern is fully integrated, the need for the cold disappears, and we stop getting sick.

This really works, and I have experienced long phases of being cold free, even when my son and husband are literally sneezing right on me. Now, I only get ill when I am missing some big lesson or trying to make things I want in my life go faster.

During the editing phase for this book, I got a doozy of a chest cold and bronchitis. Endless coughing fits were more than just a need for rest, but a deep need to be heard and noticed. It only eased when I started writing more earnestly on this beloved book of mine. I also needed to surrender my overall frustration that my business wasn't going as fast as I wanted it to. I wanted a full slate of fully booked classes, and that just wasn't happening, no matter how much I tried. Of course, with a lighter course load, I was able to dedicate more hours to writing that would, otherwise, be taken up with teaching. It was not the *circumstances* that were causing me grief, but my *attitude* towards it. As soon as I eased my interpretation of what a lower attendance meant for me, that I was given the writing time, then I got better, almost instantly.

Be grateful for and appreciative of the intuition and insight your body has for you. Appreciate the signals you are receiving from that deeper and higher wisdom. Your body is a marvelous and dynamic receiver of your intuitive vibes. Begin by listening!

Affirmation Ladder

Gratitude feels wonderful — if you are in a place you can truly experience it!

It's easy to find gratitude when you are in the midst of wonderful experiences. When things are going badly...well... gratitude is just plain annoying. The ability to be grateful in any and all circumstances is a skill that needs to be practiced.

As with other areas of your life, you can use affirmations to improve your feelings of gratitude. By starting where you are and gradually shifting to more and more positive statements, you can powerfully shift into gratitude at any time, regardless of whether or not you have what you want. Gratitude is especially powerful when you are at the limit of your coping. The less well things are going, the more important gratitude becomes.

Rate your level of gratitude on a scale from 0 to 10. Zero is feeling critical and depressed; *nothing* is good in your life. Ten is feeling you are overflowing with joy, gratitude, and appreciation; your heart is so full with all your blessings.

Honour what is happening for you, right now. Honestly assess your gratitude, without fear or judgment. There is no right or wrong here. Just start where you are, knowing your feelings can all shift in a moment. Take a deep breath. Close your eyes. Rate your gratitude level, right now.

Be gentle with yourself. You always have the choice to begin anew. You are always able to change. You need not share your current level with anyone but yourself. Be willing to let go of judgment or comparing. Being in a really low place is perfectly okay. Now you have a solid tool to shift your state — gratitude affirmations!

If you are unsure about what level of gratitude you are currently at, then just read through the affirmations below. The affirmation that 'zings' or feels closest to the truth for you is likely the level you are currently at.

Practice the affirmation that resonates as truth for you in this moment, until it feels natural. Then read upwards through the scale to the next one that 'zings'. Continue moving upwards, and you will reach ten, feeling filled with gratitude.

Don't worry if it takes you weeks or months of practicing affirmations before you feel ready to move up to the next one. It takes time to shift a lifetime of old patterns.

By practicing your chosen affirmation daily, looking into your eyes in a mirror, you will rewire your brain for gratitude. Soon, gratitude will become the new normal.

Gratitude Affirmation Ladder

10	I am tremendously grateful for all my many experiences. Life grows and expands through me! I love my life!
9	I am filled with appreciation for every aspect of my life. I am so lucky to be me!
8	I love my life. I appreciate all I have and all I am able to give. I am generous and abundant in my gratitude.
7	I am so grateful for my life, the good and the bad. I am so grateful for all my teachers, the good and the bad. Everyone is my teacher; I honour them for these lessons.
6	I appreciate my many blessings. Everywhere I look, I see love surrounding me. My gratitude increases what I see.
5	My life is getting better every day. I see miracles every time I look. I appreciate the gifts and challenges of life now.
4	The Ground below my feet, the Air above my head, these two Powers help me in so many ways every day. Thank you Earth. Thank you Sky.
3	I appreciate my ability to breathe, to read, to learn, to live. I am alive. There is hope.
2	I acknowledge the tiny glimmer of hope in the darkness. Day follows night; night follows day. I look to Nature's cycles as evidence that hope is possible.
1	My life is in crisis right now. Even though my life is currently a mess, I can acknowledge that I am alive, I can breathe, my heart is still beating.
0	My life is in chaos right now. Nothing seems to be going right for me at the moment. Even though everything is going so badly right now, I am still a good person.

Stop and Give me 5!

Start a timer for 5 minutes, right now. See your gratitude as a ball of energy swirling within your chest. As you breathe, the ball of energy grows, becomes brighter, gets bigger. See the energy ball of gratitude grow so large it fills your body and surrounds you in bright, bright, white light. This is the energy of Divine Love. When you are done, stamp your feet on the ground, shake your hands, and thank the earth and the sky.

Practice

By now, you have probably experienced the results gratitude can give you. Most of all, gratitude fills you up with positive emotion. It fuels you when times are tough. It enhances your life when things are going well. Gratitude is its own reward.

The practice of gratitude is simply to make it a daily habit. Gratitude journals are a wonderful tool to help you remember all of your blessings.

Every day, simply write a list of all the wonderful things in your life. This can include feelings, experiences, and other tangible things. You can also include people, plants, and animals you love. Make the list detailed and descriptive, with a minimum of 3 new things each day.

My examples from this moment are: the soft sounds of rain outside falling on the new green grass of spring, the cup of coffee beside me as I write, the flat of tomato and herb plants waiting to be planted in the pots on my balcony garden.

You can tell stories that inspired you, you can add photos and videos to a digital journal, you can draw or doodle your gratitude, or you can write thank you cards. Be creative and have fun adding new ways to record your appreciation.

Bonus Practice for Tough Times

Sometimes the sh#t really hits the fan in your life.

Gratitude is about the last thing on your mind.

When things are really going badly, the tendency is to become focused on the problem. Your troubles dominate your thoughts. They are all you talk about. Every moment is spent dealing with the problem or running away from it, either by physically leaving or by leaving emotionally by engaging in numbing behaviors.

It can become an endless loop. Until the problem is resolved, you are trapped in an endless struggle of worry, complaining, running, or numbing. It is important to address the issue head on and give some space for your honest feelings about it. However, continual focus on the problem does not always make the problem better, and it is mightily fatiguing. You get tired of your problems and so do all of your friends.

This gratitude practice is designed for those times, where life seems to be nothing but hardship and suffering.

Use a stop watch and time your venting about the issue. You can do this exercise by yourself or with a trusted friend. Give yourself permission to be honest about how you feel about the problem, really vent. Give voice to all of the ways this problem is really terrible. Go on! Be honest! Don't hold back. Time this venting period carefully.

When you feel like you are done, you lose steam with the process, or you begin to repeat yourself, stop the stop watch and note the time.

Now set a timer for an equal amount of time. Start the timer and list and describe all the things you appreciate about yourself, your life, and even this situation. Talk for an equal length of time about your gratitude. What is good about your life right now? What do you like? What do you love and appreciate?

It can be about anything that might give you a tiny moment of joy.

For every minute you complain and rant, you now need to spend an equal minute on gratitude.

Hmm, that changes things, doesn't it?!?

How long are you willing to discuss your problems if you know you need to follow up with an equal time spent in gratitude? How long are you willing to discuss your joy? It becomes a perfect limiter of endless ranting, because you become aware of how long you actually spend complaining. By following complaining with appreciation, you neutralize your negative attraction and become a positive magnet for what you really want.

You slow down the snowball effect, where small problems become big problems and more and more negativity comes your way. In the space of a few minutes spent in gratitude, you can slow down the problem itself, and you will begin to attract the solution. Even more important, you can receive and understand the inspired idea that solves your problem. Minute for minute, appreciation will shift everything.

Staying In the Present Is the Easiest Way to Get Through Hard Times

The venting and appreciating sessions will help soothe the intensity of whatever difficulty you are experiencing. When the s#!t hits the fan, this exercise can get you through it.

Between these releasing sessions, do your best to focus only on the minute you are in. Surrender the past and future and stay doggedly focused on the minute to minute aspects of your day. Deal with what is right in front of you. Give the present moment your full attention. This shifts you out of worry and anger and gives you some ease and rest in the midst of the chaos.

Look at the road, not at the ditch.

If you find yourself talking about the problem or endlessly ruminating about it, STOP. Actually, become completely still for a moment.

Pause.

Then go back to the releasing exercise again. Set a stopwatch and give yourself space to honestly voice your feelings. Feel and release your true emotions, without suppressing them. This allows you to take control and authority over your own emotional state; rather than having these rogue thoughts and emotions hijack your day or your life, you honestly face them. In so doing, they begin to lose their power over you.

Following up this honest voicing with an equal amount of time spent in gratitude allows you to step out of the way of your problems for a moment. In the process, you gain much needed clarity and perspective. When you get into the mindset of gratitude, it is like tuning your mind to the same frequency as the Divine. Answers and solutions will come to you in these moments.

The more you tune into the frequency of gratitude and stay focused in the present moment, the faster you will receive the insight and clarity you are looking for. Everything will begin to line up for you, and you will see order and calm returning to your life.

You did it! You shifted from wounded victim to powerful manifestor in the space of a few minutes. Huzzah!

CHAPTER SEVEN:

Do the Work

Meditation can help us embrace our worries, our fear, our anger; and that is very healing. We let our own natural capacity of healing do the work.

~Thich Nhat Hanh

The fourth Reiki Ideal is to 'do your work honestly'. In this case, the work is your meditative practice and spiritual self-care. Self-care can include affirmations, reading, giving yourself time to reflect, talking to a friend or support network about something vulnerable, receiving Reiki or other healing modalities, and of course meditation.

Self-care includes all of those things, but it can also mean doing the difficult things too, asking for more time, saying no, standing your ground, setting boundaries, doing what you are avoiding, but your soul is nudging you to do. It includes writing the book, speaking up, showing up, being brave, and most definitely being vulnerable.

To do your work honestly is to make a commitment to do the real world activities necessary to move you along your soul's path. It means to be dedicated to bringing more of your Divine essence to the world. Showing up, being willing to fail and try again is also part of the work we are talking about.

It is diving into the vulnerable and scared places to discover the gifts they hold. It is being willing to release negative patterns and thoughts that do not support you. It is seeking counseling when you are having a breakdown. It is going to your doctor and physical health team when you have an illness. It is seeking comfort from your Higher Power, when it feels like the last light has gone out.

Meditation Will Change Your Whole Life

Sitting still, in meditation, is a huge part of this work and makes all of the other actions you need to take so much easier. Meditation gives us enormous benefits, when life is going well, but it is absolutely necessary when things are falling apart.

Meditation is the rock you can cling to when everything else is in chaos. It has the power to ease emotional, physical, and spiritual pain in as little as five minutes.

Seriously.

The more often you return to meditation, the bigger the benefit. So even a tiny little meditation break will work wonders. It also works, even when you feel monkey-minded and restless. In fact, those uncomfortable and downright crappy meditations are the ones where you make the most gains in your inner contentment and happiness.

The term 'honestly' that pops up in the wording of this Reiki Ideal means you are committed and dedicated to the spirit of why you are meditating or practicing self-care. Rather than just going through the motions, this Reiki Ideal *challenges* you to *fully* show up and devote yourself.

To get the most out of any spiritual practice, you must really do it! It is not enough to follow the ritual, without the heart. When you fully *commit* yourself to any practice, *that* is when you see *results*.

What Is Meditation Really?

Meditation is mind-training.

It is a practice for coping with living in a busy and chaotic world. The more we can learn to focus only on the thoughts we choose, the better we are able to live happier and more fulfilling lives.

Meditation is simply *focus*.

It is the ability to turn our thoughts toward **any** point of focus we choose, for as long as we choose. Focus must be practiced. It is a skill that can be honed and strengthened through repetition, and **repetition** is key here.

Meditation is far more powerful when you come back to it repeatedly, each day and throughout the day.

Just 5 seconds to 5 minutes can radically transform your inner landscape. After even a short meditation, you will see immediate and tangible changes in how you see the world and how you feel in your body.

Attention and focus are trained through the practice of meditation. Meditation is the **true work** the Reiki Ideals are talking about. In order to be present to the situation we are in, we have to first learn the skill of focusing the mind upon 'wanted' thoughts. We must allow thoughts that are unwanted to slip away.

Thoughts float to us and through us, much the same way radio waves are dispersed through the atmosphere. A thought can only become conscious if we are "tuned" to it; otherwise, it just floats on by, unaffected by our presence. We have new thoughts similar to the ones we are already holding.

When we focus the mind in meditation, the goal is not to have **no** thoughts, but to **choose** the thoughts we wish to keep thinking.

Let's try it now!

Do the Work Meditation

Bring your spine up straight. Take a deep breath.

Fill your belly, your lower rib cage, and your low back with a deep breath in.

Let it all the way out.

Allow your breath to flow and fill the deepest part of your lungs. Just make space for the breath and let the air flow in with ease and grace.

If your attention wanders, just gently notice it and return it softly to this deep and smooth and peaceful breath.

Return, again and again, to your breath.

There is no forcing here, no harshness. Just be gentle with yourself. Breathe gently with the sweetness of a baby.

Returning again and again to the soft and gentle focus. Feeling the easy rhythm of your breath as it easily meets the needs of your body in this NOW moment.

Everything can change with one deep breath.

Be willing to release the need to put yourself last.

Honour where you are right now. Breathe in knowing. Breathe out resistance.

You are only a moment away from connecting to Source. It doesn't take much time, just one deep breath.

Breathing in, you are enough.

Breathing out, you are worthy.

Breathing in, you are enough.

Breathing out, you are worthy.

Breathing in, you are enough.

Breathing out, you are worthy.

You honour yourself and your worth. You meditate.

Expansion, Joy, and Peace are in each breath.

You are filled with light and with life in every breath you breathe.

Allow all good to flow to you now.

Surrender to the stillness of the soul.

Now... You are here. Every moment is a meditation.

Breathe gently. Breathe easily.

Wiggle your fingers and your toes.

Rub the palms of your hands together. Gently massage your face, head, neck, and shoulders.

Give yourself a big hug.

Your 'work' is done!

Sharing Circle

Spend the next 5 minutes writing about your experience in the meditation.

How do you feel now, compared to how you felt before the meditation?

What would change in your life if you embraced a regular meditation practice?

Meditation Will Help You Find Your Life Purpose

You align with your spirit in the moment you take one deep breath. A moment of letting go, if only for a second, allows the love of all creation to rush into your experience. It only takes a second to change everything.

Meditation, affirmations, and getting out of the way are all part of doing your spiritual work. They are all ways you are able to step aside and allow all the goodness you are, on a spiritual scale, to pour through you.

Your work is to show up to your life, to be present, to be a pure conduit of spiritual energy in the world.

Your spiritual work sets you on the path of your Dharma, your life's purpose. You need not know exactly what your Dharma is before you begin; you only need to be willing to show up and do the work each day, and the path will be revealed, step by step.

Finding your unique purpose in the world is an evolving thing. Expect it to grow and shift as you do. The surest way to follow your Dharma is to get very still, meditate, and get familiar with that settled and aware feeling. Then notice, as you go through your day, what activities are a match to that expanded and aware feeling and what activities are not.

The more you meditate, the clearer you get on what the next best step is for you in any moment. Meditation enhances your inner compass that leads you on your journey through life. It enables you to feel the wisdom and call of your heart. When you listen and act from that deep source of information, you are well on your way to making a substantial contribution to the world.

It's Not about Money, Honey! It's about the LOVE!

You may or may not receive monetary compensation for your spiritual work. Let go of the idea that the only valuable things are those with a price tag.

You are valuable, simply because you exist. Every single person enhances and uplifts the world, merely by their presence. You may never know the full impact of your kindness and gratitude has on the world until you have passed on. Your impact is already huge, and when you add daily meditation, you will be astounded by the beauty and joy you can create in your life and in the lives of others.

But You Can Also Have LOTS Of Money, Too!

Let's also just say here that you CAN be paid very well for the spiritual work you do! If your calling is to provide healing and helping services for others, you can absolutely create that. Guaranteed.

The fastest way to create a healthy and thriving business is to get still, meditate, and connect with the calling of your heart. When you let your inner compass guide you, the right people, experiences, and books will show up in your life at the exact right time.

From a stable base of meditation and self-care, you truly can accomplish anything. Not only that, having a meditation practice will help you when you DO achieve success, keeping you aligned with your best decisions, so you can continue to grow and thrive.

Time to Get To Work!

You are absolutely needed in the world right now. Your voice is needed. Your creations are needed. Your energy is needed. You are a powerful creator, and you are already helping the world SO MUCH just by being in it.

We are all interconnected with each other. When one of us shifts to a more positive place through a few minutes of meditation or other positive focus, we are immediately uplifting the energy around us. We shift the WHOLE Universe when we shift.

The energy of the Universe is naturally healing and loving. When we shift into our healthy and loving selves, we can access the whole power of the Universe. One positive energy or thought can counteract hundreds, if not thousands, of negative ones. This positive and loving energy is potent. It doesn't take much to create a HUGE effect. That is why only a few minutes of mediation a day can create such huge changes, nearly instantaneously. With mediation, you can access the power of the Universe to bring positive and loving changes in your life.

Signs of Spring

Notice the ways you are able to keep your thoughts positive. Give thanks and honour those moments as evidence you are able to Master your thoughts.

Notice the ways you slide into negativity. Give thanks and honour these moments as evidence you are now aware of what used to be an unconscious process. In your awareness, you can shift the negative to the positive.

This new awareness is a Sign of Spring and is a powerful indicator your meditation practice is working.

Self Care & Love

I am a huge lover of stationery. To me, there is nothing better than a new journal, nice paper, and colourful pens, and felts, and pencil crayons. I love doodling and colouring, creating something new, something that is all mine.

A project that I love doing with my Reiki students is to draw or illustrate the Reiki Ideals. By drawing and writing them out, you can remember them better when you really need them.

So, this is the self-care activity:

Draw or doodle the Reiki Ideals!

But first! Some rules:

1. Make it meaningful to you.

2. Put your full attention on each Ideal as you colour.

3. Allow it to be perfectly imperfect.

4. Sign and frame it.

This activity is a fun way to remember the Ideals, but it has an even larger purpose: activating your creativity.

Creativity & Self-care

Creativity is a human need. It is the best gift of being here on earth. Creativity is not limited to 'artists'; it is something everyone has within them. We all need a safe space for our creativity to be expressed and experienced.

Creativity is part of being whole. It is part of our self-care and self-expression in the world. It is part of our work. We create all the time. Any time you do anything, you are creating. When you strive to bring something new into the world, you are creating.

Creativity is valuable to the spirit, and it needs to be protected. It's a vulnerable thing to share something created from the heart. But creating and sharing our creations is as basic as it gets to being brave and vulnerable all at the same time. Creating is vulnerable. But completely worth the risk.

I think that is why so many people shut down their creativity and convince themselves they cannot dance, sing, or draw. We risk nothing if we never try.

But the costs of not trying are too high. When we shut down our creativity, several other valuable things go right along with it. Among the gifts connected to creativity are: problem solving, connection, abundance, and joy. Our sacral and throat chakras get affected, and it becomes difficult to truly express who we are in the world. When that happens, we can become distant and disconnected from others. We can feel like no one really understands us, and we begin to feel desperately alone.

I know this, because I have experienced it. I decided, at a young age, that my voice was not good at singing, my body was too short for dancing, and my hands were too unskilled for drawing, and my words were too raw and blunt for writing. I withdrew from the world and felt like only a few others really understood or cared for me. In reality, I never *shared* who I really was, so I deprived everyone of getting to know the real me.

When you retreat from joyfully creating, it quickly becomes even more scary to begin again. Any tiny criticism can send you back into hiding. Your ego voice gets echoed in the outer world, and you just see it as confirmation that you have nothing of value to bring to the world. Or worse, you decide someone else has already created it, so you don't need to.

True Art Is Merely a Record of the Transformation of Its Creator

When you are transformed by the process of doing something, what you are really creating is art.

Art has meaning. Art has purpose. It is not the job of the artist to make it have meaning for anyone else. The most influential artists and creators in the world are those who are willing to bring their unique selves to their work and risk being different.

Art is vulnerable, but ultimately, vulnerability is where human connection is born.

When we practice our art, whatever form that takes, we are actually practicing the art of connection. When I write poetry, I strive to capture a feeling or experience. I want to share what it FELT like. In so doing, I feel like I am letting other people in, letting them see and understand the real me, letting them meet me again for the first time. I also get to know myself better and put my experience in context.

You don't have to be perfect, you don't have to get it right, you don't have to impress anyone, you don't have to even show *anyone*, but you do need to create.

Don't do it well. Just do it. Over time, the 'wellness' part, the skill in expressing, it will be there too. But for now, just create.

Colour and scribble. Make it messy. Make it your own. Make a mistake. *Do* with abandon.

Intuition

When you start meditating on a regular basis, a natural result is an increase in the frequency and accuracy of your intuition. Meditation is a natural 'getting out of the way' practice, and when you are out of the way, it creates space for the Divine to enter.

Often, the focus in meditation is to quiet the mind to give ourselves some rest from rampaging thoughts. While this is a great practice, over time, the Universe notices the stillness and receptivity of your mind and will then begin to transmit messages and information for your spiritual path in life. The intuitive 'hits' you can receive in meditation are profound. No need to push away all that great information!

For me, meditation is like opening the door to the Divine. I invite the beings that are filled with love and light to join me for a conversation. I deliberately choose the beings I want to connect with. I don't leave it to chance. There are many non-physical beings out there, but not all of them are worth talking to. If you can go directly to the Source, why would you bother with anyone else?

I believe everyone can communicate directly with Spiritual beings. We all emanate from the same source energy, and we, ultimately, all return to that energy. So at our core, we have an energy vibration *in common* with the ascended masters, like Jesus or Master Usui, as well as the angels, guides, archangels, and even the Divine itself.

Any being from any spiritual practice is available to answer our questions. This also includes people we respect and admire who have passed, our ancestors and loved ones. All that is required is a little faith, belief in yourself, and a bit of meditative and visualization practice.

The faith part is you actually must believe the beings you want to talk to exist and have your best interests at heart. Divine messages are ALWAYS uplifting, inspiring, and leave you feeling good. Anything else, anything that makes you feel uncomfortable, or is critical or judgmental is likely coming from your ego or own inner critic. Source loves you unconditionally. The voice of Source is always uplifting. Go straight to the source and ask your questions.

Believing you are able to receive clear messages from Divine Beings you share a deep connection with is the first step towards receiving your guidance. Trust me; if you are reading this book, you have a deep ability to communicate to the spirit world and get meaningful and practical advice.

To access this level of intuition and spiritual communication, first, you must raise your own vibration to match the vibration of the beings you want to communicate with. The easiest way to increase the vibration of your spirit is to spend a few minutes in silent meditation. The focal point of this meditation is non-attachment. Any thoughts that might move through your experience, surrender them to the care of the Universe (God, Goddess, Divine).

You can use the following guided meditation as a starting point, but before you begin, get a pen and paper ready!

Listening to the Listener Meditation

Take a deep breath.

Become settled.

Still your body and rest.

Be willing to let it all go. Be open. Be receptive.

Access the deep, receptive quality of listening. Listen Deeply.

The Universe is the ultimate listener. It is able to witness all activities, vibrations, and thoughts that occur. Let go of any noisy or disruptive thoughts, so that you can hear the Listener.

The Universe listens.

Get in the attitude of the Listener. Become still and hear the quality of deep listening that exists in the Universe.

Breathe into the space of listening and let it expand. Let it fill your whole body.

Rest here, in this space, allowing the sensation of listening to expand gently. Stay in meditation until you feel the resonance; feel the quality of listening.

Now, when you are ready, wiggle your fingers and your toes.

Bring yourself back to your body and this present moment.

Give yourself a hug and a stretch. Your meditation is done.

Let It Go and Let It Flow!

Immediately following the meditation, write a dialog with your Higher Being, the wisest and most expanded aspect of yourself. Write to your *soul*.

You can ask your Higher Being anything you like. Any question or issue you are working on is a perfect place to start. You can also use the prompts in the next section to start, and just like a good conversation, allow the dialog to grow and develop on its own.

Allow your wise Higher Being, your soul, to respond to each question. Do not edit the response. Just let your pen flow with the answers that pop into your mind. You will know you are truly accessing your Higher Being if your answers are uplifting, insightful, and helpful.

If you get anything else, anything that makes you feel even the slightest constriction, you are accessing your ego, not your Higher Being. Anything coming from your ego is destructive and constricting to your energy. You need not obliterate the ego; just don't listen to it. Recognize it for what it is and turn your attention towards your Higher Being. If this happens to you, don't worry! Just go back to the meditation practice and spend a bit longer syncing up with your soul. Once you connect in meditation, the writing will be pure and will flow easily.

It is important to ask questions that are filled with love and integrity. If you ask a question that is not honorable or is based on a flawed assumption like, "Why am I so incompetent?", your Higher Being will tell you, right away, you are asking a bad question. They won't answer any self-destructive questions.

They will immediately steer you towards the light. They may even tell you the better question to ask.

If you bring a question to them that does not help you, they will teach you how to love yourself more. Some of them, like Jesus, can get downright feisty if they see you being mean to yourself. To them, you are a vessel of God; you are the Divine incarnate. They see your Buddha-nature and your divine potential, and they will not tolerate you being less than loving to yourself. A being of light will not let you wallow in darkness; they *always* bring you to the light.

If you have tried the meditation practice a few times, and you are still getting negative messages coming through, then you will need to seek the help of an experienced healer, Reiki Master, counselor, or physician. A being of light *will not* let you wallow in darkness. They will always guide you to a better place. You will always feel better after talking to them, and the advice is always sound. Wise and kind beings will never suggest you do anything that could harm another. They will *never* coach you towards fear, anger, or worry. If that happens when you do this exercise, there may be some deeper issues going on for you that require extra help.

Be courageous. Ask for help.

Everyone needs extra support from time to time. There is no shame in it at all. You are not bad. You always have the ability to heal and grow. Surround yourself with love and loving people with your best interests at heart.

Except in rare circumstances, the combination of meditation, the intention to sync up with the Divine, and the best, high integrity questions, will get you a *very positive* response. Trust you can connect with the Divine, because it already lives within you.

Dialogue Prompts for Writing to your Higher Being

You can use these prompts to begin a dialogue with your Higher Being or any other Divine Being. The questions will prompt the answer, so start with questions that are uplifting.

Your Higher Being and Divine Beings who love you will not answer a question of low integrity like "Why am I so messed up?" Don't even go there.

Avoid the "why" questions. They are generally not useful and can often end up unanswered if your Higher Being views them as unloving. Divine beings, including your soul, only want to talk about how wonderful you are and how they can help you. Ask "How" or "What" questions to start. Check out the prompts below. Use them as a starting point for your conversations with the Divine

How to Talk To the Divine

To begin, at the top of a blank page, write a dash (-) and your name. Then write a dot or star (*) and the name of the being you are talking to; in this case, it would be: "* Higher Being."

Use the dash and star to indicate who is talking in your dialogue. You could also switch pen colours, but I find that it slows down the process a bit. Totally up to you, though.

Write down each of the prompts in your own handwriting, as it will get you used to the dialoguing process. If you find a question opens up the dialogue, and you want to keep exploring it with the Divine being you are accessing, then go right ahead and have a great conversation! These questions are all great jumping off points for you to begin; let the conversation unfold naturally.

- *Hello Higher Being.*

* {allow the normal conversational "Hello" to emerge and write it down as you receive it.}

- *Thank you for being present here. My question for you is: How can I open up more to Divine Love?*

* {let the answer flow}

- *How can I access my creativity in a greater way?*

*

- *How can I increase my physical vitality, energy levels, and overall health?*

*

- *How can I access my spiritual power in my daily life?*

*

- *How can I learn to love myself more?*

*

- *How do I learn to live from the wisdom in my heart?*

*

- *How do I increase and expand my connection with the Divine?*

*

- *How do I learn to enjoy life more?*

*

- *What is the best way to learn more and expand my knowledge?*

*

- What do I need to know about this situation in my life that is bothering me?

*

- How do I best maintain my connection with my Divinity in the middle of my busy life?

*

- How can I be kinder to myself?

*

- How can I access more forgiveness and compassion in my life?

*

Let Go and Let God!

You may get long answers, or you might get one or two words. You might see pictures or movies. Write and draw the information as you receive it. As you continue with this process, the answers will become clearer.

Don't worry if it doesn't work right away. Sometimes all that is needed is building the trust you can access your soul's wisdom. The Divine wants to communicate with you, just as much as you do with it. Believe you can, and the rest will follow.

Try this process with Ascended Masters and Divine Beings you work with regularly. Each has their own style and personality, just as you would expect. All of them love you unconditionally and just want to help you. It is like talking with pure love.

You can also use this method to contact departed loved ones. You can let the questions be just like they were sitting in the room with you. They mostly want you to know they are not gone, they are very much alive, maybe even more alive than you, because they have access to their infinite selves. They are the highest and best parts of themselves on the other side, and they are so helpful and loving. Just remember to focus on where they are now, at one with infinite Source, rather than where they are not, in their physical body.

Any skill or talent they had in life, they also take with them. You can ask them to help you with anything, but they are really good at helping you with what they were good at in life. So, if your aunt was a successful business woman, you could ask her for business advice. If your grandma was good at gardening, you could ask which flowers to plant. If your uncle was a good judge of character, you could ask him if someone is trustworthy.

As you access the wealth of spiritual resources available to you, you will get greater and greater insight into your life. The guidance is tremendously helpful and will absolutely improve your life. The more you access it, the greater the clarity of the messages. You CAN do this, and it will absolutely change your life.

Asking for Help is Good Self-Care

As you progress through the exercises in this book, you may find old issues rising to the surface. That is a very good thing! It means it is working. Most of the time, if you apply the material you are learning, you can handle the things that come up. That is wonderful!

Sometimes, though, things come up, but they get stuck. You have done the work in recognizing an old pattern, but the last bit is still jammed in the circuits. That is when you need to ask for help.

Asking for help appropriately, at the right time, to the right person, is a skill that can take years to master. You don't need to run for help for every little thing, because you know yourself to be capable. But it is also important to know that not every situation is meant to be tackled alone. There are some big traumas that can happen in life, and they need a team approach.

If you are drawn to helping others, you must build your support team. The bigger the work, the bigger the team.

Begin to look for support professionals you trust with your spiritual, mental, emotional, and physical health. You may not need to access them very often, but you *do* need to have a backup list in mind for when things get intense.

Asking for help makes you a good helper. Brené Brown says it really clearly: If you assign judgment to asking for help, it means you are silently judging everyone you help. Yikes! Let's not do that then! Ask for help!

I see asking for help as a key spiritual exercise. It is *more* important than helping others. Asking for and receiving help is the first step in being *able* to help others. The only way to be a true healer and helper in the world is to ask for help and be honest about where you truly are.

It is tempting to present an infallible image to others you are helping. But ultimately, that is false. We *all* have challenges to overcome, and we all benefit from helping each other. It is a true gift to help another. Allow someone *else* the profound gift of helping you!

Asking for Divine help is no different than asking for help in the physical world. Opening up to divine communication is much, much easier if you can develop the practice of receiving help from others. It all goes together. If the earlier writing exercise was really hard for you, try asking for help from the people around you for anything you may need some help with, from washing the dishes to receiving a healing session. See if that enhances your intuitive ability to ask and receive help from the Divine.

Doing the Work Affirmation Ladder

Yahoo! Affirmations!!!

Use the energy of these words to move beyond shame and self-criticism that might hold you back from doing the things that nourish your soul. As you repeat the affirmation for the level you are at, you open the door to worthiness and feeling valuable and worth the time to care for yourself.

Just as with anger, worry, and gratitude, you can rate your commitment to self-care and meditation on a scale of 0 to 10. Look up the affirmation in the table below and shift your whole outlook!

Using the Affirmation Ladder

Rate your current level of commitment to your meditative or self-care work on a scale from zero to ten.

Self-care can include affirmations, being in nature, taking time for yourself, exercising, asking for help, or going for an appointment with a healing/helping professional. Self-care is the things you do to nourish your soul, your mind, your emotions, and your body.

Use the affirmations below. Look up the number you are at, and read that affirmation. You can also read upwards through the ladder and stop at the affirmation that 'zings' for you, where you feel the greatest level of truth for you right now.

Work your way up the scale, repeating the affirmations ten times or more. Keep repeating the affirmation, until you feel ease; wait until it feels true for you and then move on to the next one, further and further up the ladder.

Take your time with this process. There is great power in acknowledging your truth and releasing your resistance bit by bit.

Rate your current level of doing the work, meditating, doing self-care, nourishing your soul, from 0 to 10. Zero is you do not meditate or do any self-care at all — at its core, this is caused by a feeling of unworthiness — and ten is you are immersed in mindfulness and inner stillness.

Do your Work Affirmation Ladder

10	Now... I am here. Every moment is a meditation.
9	I allow all good to flow to me now. I surrender to the stillness of the soul.
8	I am filled with light and with life in every breath I breathe.
7	Everywhere I go, everywhere I look, I see opportunities to connect and expand.
6	Expansion, Joy, and Peace are in each breath.
5	I honour myself and my worth. I meditate.
4	Breathing in, I am enough. Breathing out, I am worthy.
3	I am only a moment away from connecting to my Source. It doesn't take much time, just one deep breath.
2	I honour where I am right now. I breathe in knowing; I breathe out resistance.
1	I am willing to release the need to put myself last.
0	Right now, I do not feel worthy of Divine Love or self-care. But I can change all that with one deep breath.

Moving Beyond Unworthiness

When I began writing this section, I thought 'not meditating' was a level zero, the opposite of meditation. But not so. Master Usui quickly corrected me! The opposite of meditation is worthlessness. Yikes!

As I pondered this, that not meditating or practicing self-care is a result of a deep sense of unworthiness, I realized it is true.

Meditation is so hugely powerful, not just for the mind and spirit, but also for the body. There is so much information available now that shows meditation alone can uplift and heal almost every aspect of your life. Even your financial situation can improve, because when you meditate, you are activating the allowing part necessary for the Law of Attraction to work easily for you.

Often, when we are not doing our work, we are blocked by our lack of self-worth. If we don't value ourselves, we often put caring for our needs last. We put everyone else and their concerns above our own, sometimes, even leaving ourselves out completely!

Meditation and personal development work always feels good when we do them. Delaying or procrastinating or forgetting to meditate results from not fully embracing your good.

While it may seem like it is accidental to 'forget' to meditate, it results directly from feelings of unworthiness. It literally only takes a moment to take one deep, mindful breath; that is meditating, and that is enough. Chances are high that, if your lack of meditating negatively affected someone else, you would show up on time, every day to your meditative practice.

Not meditating *does* impact you and your loved ones negatively! The positive feelings and results you get in meditation are profound. When you delay meditation, you are actively blocking the very thing that could help you the most. And when you are not well, you affect all the people who love you most in the world. They want you happy! ***Meditation is not optional!***

Meditation is the fastest and easiest route to changing your life. When you meditate, the life you are wishing for is within your reach. Delaying meditation is, ultimately, the same as telling the Universe you are not worthy of what you want.

If you have been procrastinating on your meditative practice till now, no need to worry. It only takes a moment to shift this habit in your life. Meditation is most powerfully practiced in a short period of time each day or throughout your day.

Longer sessions are not necessary. Nice, but not necessary. It is the *frequency* of meditation that profoundly shifts your mental habits.

Create a small commitment you can keep each and every day. Try just 5 minutes daily, at first. Notice how your life changes when you incorporate this practice. If you skip meditation because 5 minutes feels too long, then try just one minute. Make the commitment so tiny that you can keep it every day.

Work at building a consistent habit, each and every day, first. Once you have that mastered, you can add longer sessions when you need them or have the time. Twenty to forty minutes is a good length of time to add in as a weekly practice. Meditation sessions longer than 40 minutes tend to be hard on the body. I am a fan of the middle path. If you feel called to do a day of meditation, take breaks every 40 minutes or so and do some stretching and yoga asanas (postures) to refresh your body. Your body is your partner in your spiritual life, so you want to treat it kindly.

It does not matter how **long** you meditate, but **that** you meditate. The consistency of your meditation and self-care practice is what will make the biggest difference in your life. It does not matter how *long* it has been since you meditated last, it only matters that you meditated **today**.

Be willing to let go of doubt, worry, and self-recrimination when it comes to your meditative practice. Just meditate. Daily.

Just for Today... Meditate!

Meditation is its own practice. It is the commitment to daily meditation that really achieves results.

Sit and breathe.

This is the only practice that is needed.

Do not be distracted by fancy styles or needing the right cushion or the perfect room or complete silence. Just show up and allow in all the energy that is available to you. Let it flow in with your breath.

Surrender to the tremendous flow of nurturing energy trying to support you. Spend a few moments each day in stillness. Be a witness to the unending flow of Divine help and support you can access in one still and present breath. In that stillness, in that space, you create.

Daily meditation will open up all the good and grace the Universe contains, and you will be able to allow your life to become better.

When you pause in this way and allow, you not only uplift and change your life and well-being, but you are now able to make a substantial and meaningful shift in the world.

EVERYONE prospers when you take that time for yourself!
Just for today, meditate!

Stop and Give me 5!

Yes! That is right! Time to meditate. For reals! Right now!

Set a timer and allow.

Allow all the Love the Universe has for you to flow in and fill you up. Let that abundant flow of light soothe all your pain, ease all your burdens, and lighten all your troubles. Surrender resistance to this waterfall of love.

Know that you are worthy of all this and MORE!!

CHAPTER EIGHT:

Kindness

That best portion of a man's life, his little, nameless, unremembered acts of kindness and love.
*~ **William Wordsworth***

Kindness is Powerful

Kindness is the fifth and final Reiki Ideal. Being kind to yourself, others, and all living things is the final guidance on living a free and joyous life.

So what does being kind mean, anyway?

Kindness is really an active form of compassion. Kindness can have actions and behaviours connected to it, and it can also be a feeling we cultivate within ourselves. It is an attitude. It is a direction. It creates a force, a wave behind it that sweeps over the rough and rocky terrain of the soul, washing away years of burden and fatigue, with a simple gesture offered from an honest heart. Kindness creates waves of abundance in all forms. It ripples to the edges of the universe and beyond. All wise and good agents of change in the world have harnessed the transformative power of kindness to create positive change. Think of Martin Luther King Jr. or Mahatma Gandhi, they created massive, sweeping, and permanent changes in entire nations, based on non-violence, which is rooted in kindness. A simple and fundamental concept of doing to others as you would have them do unto you. It is a radical thought.

Kindness is radical. Kindness has the power to change everything.

Forget being nice; be kind instead. Being kind is not about over-giving or martyrdom. Kindness must include everyone, including yourself. You cannot over-give, to the point of putting yourself in chronic disadvantage, and still call it kindness. Kindness is being gentle with yourself and others in thought, word, and deed.

Contrary to being "nice", kindness is not based on complying with social norms or keeping others happy. Being nice is about offering a behaviour to appease the needs of another. Often, being nice is about approval seeking from the level of the ego. We offer behaviours in the guise of niceness to extract a positive emotion from others.

Being nice and being kind are not the same. We can experience people who are nice on the surface, yet are seething with anger underneath, waiting like a viper for a chance to cut us down. This is not kindness. Kindness does not require us to serve others, without a thought for our own well-being. We do not have to be pleasing to another person or offer actions to get a certain result to be kind.

What Do We Have In Common?

All life is interconnected. This basis for compassion is rooted in our DNA. We may not share specific genes with other life forms, but the basic building blocks of life, DNA itself, is shared among all living things. DNA, proteins, cellular structures are all shared features; no matter if it is a human or a fly, these things we share.

When we have something in common with another, when we recognize ourselves in another, then we have the basis of compassion and kindness.

As a biologist, I see life and nature as one large spectrum of living beings. There is tremendous diversity of life on planet earth. But even with the phenomenal diversity, there are elements that are shared across all species. When we add to our understanding by acknowledging all of these diverse life forms, insects, worms, beetles, fish, spiders, butterflies, monkeys, parrots, penguins, all of them, are living on one planet.

One planet.

One planet, so far, unique among the galaxy of stars, that hosts life. We are *truly* all in this together. When we look for that basis of commonality, no matter how slight, we find the origins of compassion and kindness.

The ability to recognize distinctions and groupings of objects is a human trait. So too, we can redefine the boundaries of what 'group' a person, plant, or animal belongs to and look for what we have in common.

So much of our effort in science and our current understanding of the world has been focused on what makes one thing *different* from another. This is reductionism. Historically, the approach to understanding how something works has been to take it apart, dismantle it, and to reduce everything down to its component parts.

This reductionist model of understanding the world has been helpful in some ways, and great inventions and under-standing of the world has arisen from it. However, we are currently faced with many problems in our world that are a direct result of this narrow focus. We have lost sight of the forest. We have been so focused, not even on the trees, but on each cell on the leaves. Many environmental catastrophes could have been averted if a basic shift of perception had occurred.

Recognizing what we have in common has never been more important. We need to activate kindness and compassion in ourselves. When we do that, when we light our hearts with the flame of kindness, we can illuminate the whole world.

But first, we have to start within.

The Diversity of Life is Common to us All

I have spent the better part of my adult life studying ecology, the science of interactions. Living beings interact with each other and their environment; this is ecology. The natural world is interconnected. Everything is connected, every species, every rock and bump. There is life all over the place too. From the top of the highest mountain to the depths of deep sea vents, there is life. And where there is life, there is a web of constantly changing interactions of individuals, populations, species, and communities of plants, microbes, and animals.

Last time I checked, humans are life too.

A very big problem with our current understanding of the natural world is that we view ourselves, humans, as outside of nature. This is a *giant* mistake.

We are inextricably linked with nature. We live on Earth. That means, we live in Nature too. We are not separate or outside of the world we live in. We are at home. Here, on one planet. One planet.

One planet, unique in the galaxy.

This is all we have.

We are within the system we are studying. We change the system every time we change. But, the system, Nature, is still here, within us and around us.

The natural world as a whole would benefit immensely from one simple shift in thought. We humans are part of Nature.

We ARE nature.

We are just one species within the millions and millions of other species that are also here, sharing our planet.

Humans are a unique species, yes, but really, we are just clever apes. That is all. We are only one species within this huge web of life. When we understand how much we owe our continued existence as a species to all of the other species around us, we begin to see how our survival depends on us being respectful of ALL life on this planet.

Kindness and compassion are crucial to human survival through the next century. Not only because war has become more and more dangerous with nuclear, chemical, and biological weapons, but also our climate, watersheds, groundwater, air quality, and even the stability of our food resources depend on the continued preservation of the natural world. Kindness is not some superficial bonus. It is necessary and required. Kindness is a human need and a human right.

So yeah, kindness is a big deal.

It is huge. I'll start out by talking about what makes your continued existence possible on the planet, the continued functioning of the ecosystem. Don't worry. I'll circle back to why this all matters to you when you are dealing with a-holes.

Kindness will Save the World

I am quite passionate about the natural world. I am in awe of it. The magnificence and diversity of life is truly astounding. I often wondered why other people do not always share this deep reverence and respect for nature, especially since we cannot live here long, without that basic respect.

The survival of the natural world and our survival as a species is one and the same. Why would anyone put their survival in jeopardy for a short-term pleasure or gain?

It's like sinking the ship you are sailing in. It doesn't make any logical sense.

From my studies and observation of the choices people, governments, and big companies make about the environment, I see one common theme. It all comes down to love. Self-esteem, self-love, or the lack of it, are the basis of many nonsensical choices people make about the environment.

If a person does not care for themselves, then they will have a hard time caring about anything else. Even if they are destroying the earth on which they depend, they will not make a new choice, until they care about themselves.

This capacity to care is fundamental to our survival as a species. We need to care for ourselves, first. After that, it is easy to care for other humans and other species. It is an inside-out problem. Even though the effect is external — climate change, habitat loss, extinction — the source of the problem is a basic lack of care. And the source of that lack is a lack of self-love.

Until more people can learn to love themselves, a deep and lasting solution to the world's environmental problems is a hard struggle. Once self-love is commonplace, environmental problems will find easy solutions.

This might seem like a tangent, an interesting side bar in this book, but it is fundamental to the discussion of kindness. I believe kindness is the same as caring about the environment. If you are not kind to yourself, then it is nearly impossible to be kind to another. If anyone is unkind to you, then they are also unkind to themselves, regardless of their outer demeanor.

Being kind is hugely important. We are living in a time when being kind is no longer optional. Being kind cannot be reserved for only those we like or solely for other people and never ourselves. Learning to be kind is the single most important thing you will ever do for yourself, for others, and for the world.

The power of kindness cannot be overstated. The solution to world-wide problems, like hunger, poverty, epidemics, war, genocide, and environmental disasters, is not to be found within each separate issue. The true and deep cause of all of those outer manifestations is a lack of kindness and self-love.

The only way to truly change the world is to start within. To start with us. To start with ourselves.

It is not possible or needed to change the hearts and minds of every person on the planet. Great change always comes from within first. Trying to convince another of anything is totally missing the point. It is ourselves we need to start with! You need to start with YOU. I need to start with ME. Only ourselves.

If everyone loved themselves a little bit more and showed themselves kindness, the momentum of all the problems in the world would stop. It would stop quickly too. In time, the problems would reverse and many of the unsolvable problems would be history. Dusty history.

Start Here!

The only place we can start to change the world is with ourselves. Once we have mastered the art of self-kindness, we can extend our care and attention to others.

Often, we rush to care for everyone else first. We leave ourselves last.

This is completely backwards. We must always start with ourselves. Nurturing and caring for our innermost needs first is important before we turn to the outer world. Just as Gandhi said, "We must be the change we wish to see in the world", we need to embrace this idea and make it a part of our daily habit.

I think everyone would like to see greater kindness in the world. The absolute best place to start, likely the ONLY place to start, is with ourselves.

Moms and Dads need self-kindness too

In the case of parents, where your entire day might be tending to your little one's needs, you must take some time each and every day to care for yourself, to extend the same kindness and nurturing toward yourself as you do for your little ones. Imagine how differently your day would go if you were truly kind to yourself first.

This is important not just for you, but also for them. They are watching you closely. They are paying attention to how you treat yourself, so they will know how they must, one day, treat themselves.

If you always put yourself last, you are teaching your children to put themselves last. If you don't like yourself, your children will grow to not like themselves. If you criticize yourself, then one day, you will hear your words from your children's lips.

You owe it to them, our precious ones, to take care of yourself, today. This self-care is kindness, not just for you, but for them too.

You teach self-love and kindness by demonstrating it. Words don't matter. Actions matter. Children witness and mirror your actions. By treating yourself kindly, you are doing the single most important thing for the future of the world — raising kind and loving children.

Signs of Spring

Kindness is Attractive.

Take note of inner signs of kindness reflected in the world around you. Notice all of the ways, large and small, the Universe is kind to you.

Honour your inner being with a quick note of kindness and gratitude.

Kindness is the Basis of All Spirituality

Kindness is caring for the well-being of another and behaving in a way that benefits everyone (including you!). Kindness and compassion are spiritual qualities. Kindness is active compassion. True kindness springs from. compassionate thoughts.

Kindness and compassion are not meant to be reserved only for friends and family or only offered to those you 'like'. True compassion is offered to everyone. Even your mortal enemies are worthy of kindness and compassion. Even those who **never** offer a kind or compassionate behaviour, even those difficult ones, are worthy of kindness.

Keep in mind, this is not about being foolhardy. This is not offering the keys of your home to a drug addict because they need a place to stay. True kindness is driven by the best outcome for **all**. It does not require grand acts or outrageous generosity or thoughtless selflessness. Kindness only requires you recognize yourself in another.

Compassion challenges you to search for something the same between you and the object of your compassion. When you truly acknowledge we are all more similar than we are different, then we can act with more genuine kindness for ourselves and for others.

We are just as deserving of the kindness we offer others as they are. Begin today to behave kindly towards yourself. When you do, you will begin to naturally be kind to others.

Dismantle Shame and Unworthiness with Kindness

Kindness seems to be at odds with belligerent behavior, but it actually goes much deeper than that. Whether the lack of kindness is directed towards yourself or another, the basis is a lack of self-worth.

Unkind behaviour originates from a deep sense of unworthiness and shame.

If you have not yet heard of Brené Brown and her work on shame and vulnerability, go Google it, right now!

Seriously! It is *that* good!

She speaks powerfully about the role of shame to freeze us in our negativity. Shame, she describes, is like being stuck in a swamp. You get sucked in and dragged down. When shame runs the show, kindness is scarce.

Shame convinces us we are inherently unworthy. This deep pit of unworthiness is a trap that keeps us perpetually stuck. If we feel unworthy or shameful, then we exhibit behaviours and thoughts that create more reasons to feel shame and unworthiness.

Our shame-beasts cleverly collect only the most damaging aspects of our experience and block out all else. This destructive pattern can be directed outwardly, towards others, or inwardly, towards ourselves. Either way, the damage can be immense.

It is only when we do the inner work necessary to identify shame as the false voice it is, we begin to change. People are amazingly resilient, and you are too. You can deconstruct shame and unworthiness by deliberately building a kindness and compassion practice.

Unworthiness can be dismantled through the use of affirmations. Deep reflection on kindness and compassion also contributes to this process of healing. Just by focusing attention on kindness and compassion, it begins to powerfully shift your internal state. This inner work is incredibly important if you want to cultivate a stable and long-term sense of happiness.

The energy of kindness is not compatible with the energy of shame. The two energies literally cannot inhabit the same space. And kindness is far, far stronger. Even a tiny bit of kindness, just merely thinking about it, as you are now, will begin shifting a lifetime of unkindness, unworthiness, and shame.

Doing the inner work necessary to shift inner destructive patterns pays off, because it shifts the outward pattern. When you are willing to be kind to yourself, you immediately shift the energy around you. Your energy signature shifts, and that changes how the Law of Attraction affects you. You will find you are no longer surrounded by cruel or critical people. When you are nice to yourself, they cannot stay. There is no energetic room for them in your life.

You do not need to tolerate abuse on any level, even if it originates within your own mind. We are often far more cruel to ourselves than we would *ever* be to another. This inwardly directed cruelty can cause us to behave in a manner we would normally never consider. Our negative behaviors towards others then become a breeding ground for shame, keeping us stuck in an abusive cycle. In order to truly be kind to others, we must start with ourselves first.

Of course, that doesn't mean you can go around beating others up and be nice to yourself at the same time! We are all inter-connected. Whatever we do to another, we do to ourselves. Very often, though, people are *exceedingly* kind to others, but they are mean as heck to themselves!

This is not cool, man. Not cool!

You have my permission to treat yourself with at least much kindness as you would a stranger. It all is connected! Being kind outwardly *and* inwardly is needed. When you are kind to yourself, you are naturally kind to others.

But — What about all those cruel SOBs?

Right. So, what about all the people in the world committing unspeakable acts of cruelty? What about murderers, rapists, and genocide leaders? How does that fit in with kindness?

How do you find compassion for people who have done horrible things?

These are the heaviest of questions.

Really.

And there are no easy answers.

Finding compassion for people who are void of compassion is one of the most difficult tasks in any spiritual tradition.

'Forgive them, for they know not what they do.'

Man!

That is hard.

All I can offer is how I approach this challenge in my own practice.

The first thing I do is stop using shame language when I talk about the person.

Shame says, "You are bad."

That statement attaches 'bad' to the person's identity. They can never escape their identity. They are stuck. Always being bad. Never changing. Always bad.

I also recognize that when I label another as 'bad', my inner critic views this as a carte blanche permission slip to start labelling me as 'bad' too, even for the tiniest infraction. Shame is a slippery slope. For me, I can't use shame language for another person (even if justified) and get away without it backfiring. I do my best to label the *behaviour* as 'bad' and not the person.

The behaviour is bad. The person is the person.

I don't let them off the hook for their behaviour. There is still responsibility and making amends that ideally happens. But, I allow the person to change. If things had gone differently for them in their lives, they probably would have made better choices.

I do my best to understand their early childhood experiences, mental disorders, social conditions, injuries, or illnesses they might have had. I try to understand the whole story, not just the headline.

Ask, "What on *earth* happened to them that made them do that horrible thing?"

When you look for that answer, you often uncover mountains of misery, often extending back generations.

At the very least, they were once a helpless infant, just like me. At some point, something went wrong for them. This does not excuse their behaviour, but it helps me understand it a little bit better.

If I can get even a tiny bit of compassion going for them, it makes me better able to think about what could be done to prevent further cruelty. Compassion brings creative solutions to very tough problems.

Sometimes, in really horrible events, the best I can do to feel compassion for the perpetrator is to know the damage they are doing to their soul by harming another. That stuff can take lifetimes to repair. It is very heavy work and a very hard karmic road ahead for them. The compassion I feel for them is profound sadness that they might go centuries before feeling the warm light of Divine love on their faces. I always hope they will turn towards the light.

This sort of compassion building for people I hear about in the news or in history books is not some trivial exercise for me. Nor is it completely selfless. I benefit when I find compassion for a person who has done something terrible. If I can feel compassion for them; I can feel compassion for myself.

My inner critic used to be horribly mean to me. Often exaggerating my faults and focusing obsessively on all my problems, the shame-voice used to be so loud. By building my compassion muscle, I was able to silence my inner critic, so the voice of love, the Divine, could be heard.

Meditation

This meditation increases your capacity for kindness for yourself and others.

Grant yourself the time and space to do this meditation. Just simply making **time** for your innermost needs is a tremendous act of kindness.

Kindness Meditation

Breathe deeply.

Breathe gently.

Let your breath gently meet the needs of your body.

Get softer.

Softer.

Allow all the tension of the day to settle.

You have done all you can.

Now, it is time to meditate.

Breathe deeply in, to the count of 4.

Breathe deeply out, to the count of 8.

Just gently counting.

Observing the quality of your breath.

Observe as you breathe in, 1... 2... 3... 4...

And out, 1... 2... 3... 4... 5... 6... 7... 8...

Again, In, 1... 2... 3... 4...

And out, 1... 2... 3... 4... 5... 6... 7... 8...

Perfect.

Well done.

Keep going.

You are doing so well.

You are doing so well in this meditation; you are doing so well in everything. You are willing to show up and be here, in this space.

Resting in the awareness of your breath.

In, 1... 2... 3... 4...

And out, 1... 2... 3... 4... 5... 6... 7... 8...

That is all you need to do right now.

Right now, that is enough.

You are enough.

You are loved.

You are loving.

You are worthy.

You are worthy of love.

Your love is appreciated.

Thank you for the love you bring to the world.

Breathe gently.

Breathe easily.

Remain in meditation as long as it feels nourishing to you.

Namaste.

Sharing Circle

Spend the next 5 minutes writing about your experience in the meditation.

How do you feel now, compared to how you felt before the meditation?

How have your feelings of kindness toward yourself changed?

Self Care & Love

In many ways, kindness is following the golden rule, do unto others as you would have them do unto you, but with the adjustment of including yourself in the kindness. Care for yourself as you want others to care for you. Care for yourself as much as you care for others.

The Kindness Paradox

Kindness carries the same energy signature as the Divine. Divine Energy can flow with all the power and grandness of a lightning bolt, but it can also be profoundly gentle, like a whisper, a flutter of energy through your fingers, like a soft breeze on a hot day.

Kindness in your life is a lot like this. Sometimes, kindness looks like softly touching a baby's cheek as you gaze in their eyes. Sometimes, kindness is yelling at an abuser to stop. Sometimes, kindness is telling ourselves to stop; stop repeating the words that have been unkindly spoken to us.

The abuser may say something only once, but we perpetuate inner violence when we repeat the negative and derogatory statements within our minds. The inner critic must be told, firmly, unequivocally, "NO!"

No more. No more lies. No more comparing. No more approval seeking. No more inner dialogue about how bad we are and how much we have failed and are failing and will always fail. No!

The paradox of kindness is that it is sometimes forceful, loud, and brash. But it is still kindness if the intention is centered on compassion. Being meek and mild all the time is not kind if it means people are stomping all over your boundaries.

Kindness includes everyone, including you. If you are being 'nice' to others at the expense of your own well-being, you are no longer being kind.

Kindness, Compassion in Action

But what does it mean to be kind to yourself?

It means you take the day off work, when you are soul-weary.

It means you refrain from criticizing anyone for anything. Pointing out flaws only entrenches inner critical thoughts.

Kindness means clothing yourself nicely and caring for your physical body.

Kindness is taking yourself on a me-date and buying yourself flowers and something delicious.

Kindness is giving up comparing yourself to anyone else for any reason. Comparing is just another way to put ourselves or another down. Neither is beneficial to your well-being or your soul.

Kindness is resting when you are sick, injured, or tired, rather than pushing on and forcing yourself to use your last energy reserves on fulfilling someone else's ego needs.

Kindness is being willing to dive into the scary places in your body-mind, because you know there is healing work to do.

Kindness is turning on the lights when you are scared. It is looking for the glimmer of hope, no matter how small, and letting that hope lift you up.

Kindness is staying on the phone a few minutes longer to offer words of encouragement and praise and thanks.

Kindness is looking in your own eyes, softly, with love.

Kindness is gentleness, and it is also firm resolve.

It is kindness to tell someone no, when they have gone too far and taken too much.

It is kindness to speak up for yourself or others when it is needed.

It is kind to ferociously protect the vulnerable and the defenseless.

It is kind to bravely follow your own dreams out of the door and into the world.

It is kind to share your creativity with others.

It is kind to carefully choose your words to convey your message with the best intent.

Kindness is all of those things and so much more.

Following the kind path requires us to surrender our ego and follow the higher path. It means to look for the best outcome for all involved and to steadily make your way there.

Be a Warrior-Protector for your Inner Child

There is a pure light within you. There is something innocent and wondrous and precious. This pure light is your inner child, your child-self, your inner joy and playfulness.

This is the part of you that can remember nursery rhymes when you see a ladybug, or the part of you that picks up pennies for good luck, or the part of you that skips inside when you hear the melody of an ice cream truck, or the part that loves stirring up fall leaves and crunching them as you walk, or the part that loves the crick crack breaking of hollow ice next to the sidewalk in winter. This is the part of you that can still wonder at the green shoots poking their way through the soil, raising their sleepy heads to the sun. And it is the part of you that notices butterflies and dragonflies and songbirds. This is the most tender, precious, vulnerable part of ourselves, the part that can still wonder.

Even if you didn't have adults around you that protected you as a child, you can begin today to protect that inner little one. Create a safe space within you, where you are allowed to be joyful and playful. Give yourself permission to dream and wonder and learn, just for the joy of it. Give yourself the time and space to do playful and nurturing activities. Create safe boundaries for this space and protect it from the inner critic and the outer critic. Give this joyful part of you more room to play and have fun. Devote some time, just as a good parent does, to the enjoyment of simple things from a fresh perspective.

Just for Today — Honour Your Little YOU

Just for today, honour the part of you that still feels wonder.

Be a caretaker of this little inner one, today. Indulge in some simple joys, whatever that means to you.

Remember what you loved to do when you were little? Play with cars? Swing on the swings? Play in the garden? Pet cats and dogs? Build with blocks? Take stuff apart? Play dress up? Pretend with dolls? Jump rope? Run? Toss a ball around? Juggle? Whistle? Play tag?

Pick one activity and do that today. Follow the joy. Be kind and nurturing to your little-self. Feed yourself nourishing foods. Do something for fun. Speak kindly to this innocent and wondrous part of yourself.

Listen carefully to the wisdom of this joyous and connected-to-Spirit-aspect of yourself. At the end of the day, climb into bed, read a bedtime story, turn out the lights and say, "I love you little one! Sweet dreams!"

Intuition

When we begin to open up to our intuition, there may be a phase when we have trouble distinguishing between a valid warning signal and ego-based fear. Ego-based fear comes from our inner critic, the shame-voice in our head that berates us for every mistake and misstep. Ego fears are not real. They distract us from our best course of action, because to grow, often means to risk vulnerability. When we are willing to be vulnerable, we are able to connect, inspire, and create. Right when we are poised to make our biggest leap forward, our ego-fears can pop up and drag us right back down.

Now, it is healthy and normal to have some fear arise, due to the presence of an **actual** threat. We **want** this clarity with our intuitive muscle; we need clear and accurate warnings of **real** danger. But ego-based fear is not helpful and can keep us stuck in our pain or muddled in indecision. Thankfully, there are easy ways to tell these two flavours of fear apart!

The ego is entrenched in its stance of protecting the mental status quo at all costs. The ego keeps change to a minimum by generating false fear, a fear not grounded in reality. Ego-based fear will tell us to stop, when we really need to keep going. It will tell us to keep going, when we really need to stop.

The ego kicks up the biggest fuss when we are closest to changing, when we are closest to our true nature. It fusses and screams like an uncontrollable toddler, who needs attention. The ego is not to be trusted and not to be listened to, as it, just like a tantruming two-year-old, cannot see the wisdom of the choices of your Higher Being. The ego isn't bad; it is just misguided.

The ego is a self-protective mechanism that gets developed when we are coping with negative experiences when we do not yet have the emotional or mental ability to understand them.

When we are children, we absorb the negative thinking of our parents, teachers, and society. The ego is where the scared, lost, and shame-filled parts of ourselves collect.

I do not advocate trying to eradicate the ego. A combative approach rarely works, especially where the ego is concerned. The ego thrives on conflict and drama, so it just gets further entrenched the more hostile we are to it.

Love, however, tames the ego. The ego cannot withstand the onslaught of kindness and compassion. As soon as thoughts of kindness enter, the ego starts to leave. It has no place to stay and nowhere to hide.

The tantruming two-year old concept of the ego has been a very useful image for me. I can love a two-year old in pretty much all circumstances. Despite the raging, the kicking, the screaming, I still understand that a two-year old is only doing these things because they lack the words and the emotional maturity to choose better. I can love them through all of that, even if it is exhausting and embarrassing.

Just simply acknowledging, that my ego does not have the ability nor the skill to know all the information my Higher Being does, helps to shift things. The ego is not able to know all of the wisdom that spirit can hold. And so, it is easy to be kind to the ego and have patience with myself, when old emotional patterns or negative thoughts creep in. I can recognize it for what it is, and when I do, the ego loses its hold on me, and I get clarity. It is just a tiny child asking for attention.

Connect to Divine Love to Boost your Intuition

Intuition, accurate intuition, happens when we are able to set aside thoughts that are from the ego and enter union with the Divine Mind. We merge our individual minds with the cosmic mind and interpret the information we receive.

Information sourced from the Divine feels wonderful. Since the Divine is ecstatic energy, the better we feel, the easier it is to communicate with the Divine. It is just as simple as shifting our vibration to the level of kindness and love. Then we can get increasingly clearer and frequent intuitive hits.

The easiest way to tell the difference between Divine messages and ego messages is the way you feel. The Divine ALWAYS feels good; even when you are receiving warnings, it is loving in its attitude, and you feel relief. The ego ALWAYS feels bad. It is restriction, constriction, and fear. Often, the ego is more concerned with keeping things the same and not rocking the boat than it is concerned with your well-being and happiness.

The best practice for increasing your intuition is to be kind to yourself. As you treat yourself kindly, you are able to enhance your vibration. The Universe is not only better able to 'hear' you and your positive intentions, but you are better able to hear the Universe. The messages are clearer, easier to understand, and easier to put into practice when you are kind and gentle with your body, mind, and spirit.

The Universe loves you. Unconditionally.

EXACTLY as you are.

The Universe loves you and every pound you are, overweight or not. It loves every mistake; it loves every slip, fail, and fall. It loves you, regardless of your accomplishments or accolades. You do not earn this love; you just get it — as you are — in this moment.

When you attempt to hold the same loving attitude toward yourself, as the Universe holds for you, you are immediately on the same wavelength as the Universe. Divine messages just float in. It all becomes so easy and so very clear.

Just for Today — Get a Glimpse of God

Spend a few minutes, right now, turning your attention to the love the Universe has for you. Feel how the Universe feels about you. Let your resistance sit aside. Allow the love that is available to you fill you.

Feel it. Immerse yourself in the flow of energy and radiance that is yours.

Seek to get a glimpse of the mind of God.

God loves you! The Divine loves you! You are loved and appreciated and beautiful. You are cherished and adored. Feel this now.

Sharing Circle

What is your experience with Divine Kindness?

What miracles, tiny or profound, have you heard about or witnessed?

How does it feel to think that you are loved more than your capacity to feel or comprehend?

Stop and Give me 5!

Explore the love the Universe has for you in this moment. Exactly as you are.

Set a timer and practice letting this love all the way in. Let the light and energy of the Universe fill every space within you, every cell.

Breathe this universal support into the deepest parts of you.

Become illuminated in Divine Light and Love.

Signs of Spring

Tiny acts of kindness.

Write down your experience of kindness at work in your life.

Note the outer kindnesses, like a stranger holding the door for you, a friend calling when you need it, or an offer of help.

Also, note the inner kindnesses, like smiling in your eyes in the mirror, taking care of your body, or kind inner talk and feelings of self-love and self-esteem.

Affirmation Ladder

Rate your current level of kindness, to yourself and others, on a scale of 0 to 10. Ten is feeling and acting completely kind to every living thing and also to yourself. Zero is feeling and acting with hate or cruelty toward yourself or others.

Be easy about this. It is okay to be wherever you are. Know that you can be honest here, because you are able to change.

Practicing the affirmation that resonates with where you are now is more important than trying to jump ahead to a higher level on the Affirmation Ladder.

You will get bigger and more permanent shifts in your body-mind if you are honest. Honesty is just another form of kindness.

Kindness Affirmation Ladder

10	Kindness within me. Kindness all around me. I am kind and loving.
9	I love myself the way I am. I am kind and gentle.
8	I love myself; therefore, I am kind. I am kind; therefore, I am love.
7	I am kind and gentle with me. I am kind and gentle with others.
6	The soft breath of kindness enters my heart. I allow kindness to be my way.
5	Each moment, I am kind. Each moment I breathe, I am kind. Every moment I begin again.
4	I'm giving myself a break. I'm cutting myself some slack. I'm choosing kindness and peace over suffering and self-punishment.
3	I ask now for the courage to find kindness in my heart. God/Divine/Goddess, please help me.
2	Each moment, day by day, I make reparations and amends for my past behaviour. Each moment is a new moment. I can choose peace.
1	Unkind thoughts and words have been my pattern, but I can change. I can choose to be kind.
0	I have been cruel and mean to myself or others. Even though my behaviour was wrong, I can choose differently, starting now. I am still a good person.

You NEVER Have To Accept Abuse in Any Form

Let me be absolutely clear, being kind does NOT mean accepting abuse in *any* form. You do not need to be gentle to be kind. You can be kind AND firm. You do not need to stand for any form of emotional, physical, sexual, or spiritual abuse from anyone at any time for any reason.

Once is one time too many.

Withstanding abusive behaviour is not wise or safe or kind to yourself. Ultimately, you are worthy of being treated with kindness; if the people around you are unkind, cruel, or abusive to you, you have every right to leave.

Yes, that is right. Leave.

It doesn't matter if they are a spouse, a parent, a friend, co-worker, or boss. You have the 100% right to choose who gets to spend time with you. There are so many kind and loving people out there; you do not need to waste another second on someone who consistently disregards your safety, emotional well-being, or reasonable boundaries of how you deserve to be treated.

If you are in the middle of a violent relationship or a relationship that could turn violent, please get help from your local distress centre or the domestic violence branch of your local police service. You may need help to leave safely. There is support out there on how to do this, and you will probably need some help building your plan to leave.

Please know that, if you are in an abusive relationship, you need not pack shame in your bags when you leave. You can safely leave behind any thoughts you deserved this treatment. It is not your fault. You DO NOT deserve this. You ARE NOT bad. You are just in a bad situation. And you have the power, freedom, and resources to leave this situation safely. Begin the process by reaching out to someone safe for support.

Sometimes kindness can appear harsh. It might be saying NO and standing your ground, setting boundaries and appropriate limits on behaviour. If someone is doing something that is not cool with you, you have a responsibility (and a right) to tell them.

This boundary setting is important for you, but it is also important for the other person. Someone who has never had boundaries with others, perhaps, because they were raised without them, they will not be able to learn about acceptable behaviour, unless they have someone tell them NO and stand by it. Someone who has trouble following through on their choices is not helped by you taking them back after they left you. Someone who is rude is not helped if they are not told of their rudeness.

It may be uncomfortable to be kind in this way, speaking up and telling people clearly what is okay with you and what is not, but it is important for both you and for them. Being outwardly 'nice' to others at the expense of your own well-being is **not** true kindness. When you abandon your own need for kindness, you deprive others of necessary learning opportunities, and you also perpetuate unkindness within yourself.

Stop and Give me 5!

Put your hands over your heart.

For the next five minutes, as you breathe gently, allow the kindness, compassion, and love the Universe has for you fill you up.

Yes, another five minutes of letting in the love!

You deserve it. Simply existing makes you worthy of this deep and pure Divine Love.

Practice

Kindness is a spiritual practice.

It is easy to be kind to others, when they are also being kind. But just as with compassion, kindness cannot be reserved only for those we like. Being kind to those who seemingly 'don't deserve it' is a deeply spiritual practice.

Ultimately, everyone in our experience is a reflection of an inner part of ourselves. When we see something we don't like in another, we are only able to see this negative quality, because it exists in us as well. Even if it is just a flicker of a shadow of that negative quality, we have that quality inside. We have within us the ability to be tremendously kind and terribly awful. It is only through the power of choice we can guide our lives to kindness.

If we do the work to accept these shadow qualities within ourselves, people with these same qualities stop bothering us. When we love and accept ALL of us, even the uncomfortable and prickly parts, we have access to that same love and acceptance for others. Conversely, if we find ourselves confronted with obnoxious, annoying people, then they are giving us a valuable opportunity to love that obnoxious and annoying part within us.

When we are unkind to another, regardless of the reason, we are really just being unkind to the part within us that resembles the other person. To be unkind to another is to be unkind to ourselves.

If you criticize another, the person who hears it the most clearly is YOU. Your subconscious mind cannot differentiate between an external comment and an internal comment.

I have seen this over and over, and perhaps, you have too; the people who are most critical to others are brutal towards themselves. They can never be good enough for their inner critic. In the midst of their self-hatred, they direct some of it outward on the people around them.

Just for Today — Put Kindness into Action

Be kind to yourself.

Be kind to others.

Be kind to every living thing.

Just for today, consider how you are kind to others. How can you be kinder?

Consider how you are kind to yourself. How can you be kinder?

Choose one small act of kindness for yourself. Choose one small act of kindness for another.

Do both acts of kindness today.

CHAPTER NINE:

Grounding

Look deep into nature, and then you will understand everything better.

   ~ Albert Einstein

Connecting to the Earth

Alongside the Reiki Ideals, there are several other practices that have radically transformed my life and the lives of my students. Grounding is one the first things I teach in Reiki, but it is a powerful skill that anyone can do.

Grounding is simply connecting to the vast love of Mother Earth and allowing this energy to support and heal us.

Earth Energy is Love

Mother Earth has a vast reserve of energy and love for us. This deep and eternal love is available to us all, without judgment and without reserve. You do not need to be perfect to earn this love; you do not need to recycle to earn this love. She just loves you. She loves you just the same.

This ever-present, abundant, and kind Earth Energy is available to all who call upon it. Earth Energy is inherently healing. We can feel this healing power whenever we are outside in the fresh air or surrounded by plants, flowers, trees, or forests.

Earth energy is yin, on the yin-yang, passive-active, spectrum. It is low, like the ocean. It gathers energy to it with the ease of gravity. This energy forms a vast resource that can be accessed strongly by focusing our thoughts and being aware of the energy in the Earth. Just simply this awareness is enough to begin the energy flow.

The energy of the Earth can be soft and gentle; it can be powerful and strong. It responds to what is needed by the Law of Least Effort. The yin nature of this energy means it responds best to surrender, rather than force. You have access to greater amounts of Earth energy when you *allow* it to flow to you, rather than trying to force it or suck it up like through a straw.

Earth Energy is able to wash away emotional toxins from the body. Strong emotions are immediately soothed. Simply being in Nature is healing. Simply being aware that we are ALWAYS in Nature is healing.

This deep and pure and stable energy is necessary for energy work, like Reiki. Earth Energy connects us to the physical world and provides a stable base for us to explore the spiritual world safely. This energy gives balance and stability to our daily lives.

Earth Energy refills and replenishes us each night when we sleep. We lie horizontally and let go of our daily concerns. We allow all our systems to rest and in this rest, we are renewed.

That is the power of the Earth. If we let it, it can heal everything. We rely on the Earth for our air, water, and food. Our very lives are indebted to Mother Earth. She is ours, and we are hers. She has the powerful ability to nurture all our ills and soothe all our worries.

Just a 5-minute walk outside at lunchtime can completely renew and replenish you, especially if you bring to conscious awareness the healing energies of the Earth. Looking for nature, wherever you find it, and being aware of the beauty, no matter how small, is a deeply spiritual practice.

Enlightenment is Found in Nature

Every major religion has a story of spiritual enlightenment occurring in nature. Jesus went to Galilee, Moses to the hills, Mohamed (peace be upon him) went to the mountain, Buddha to Deer Park and the Bodhi tree. Nature is brimming with spirituality.

There are stories of countless others, who have also had great awakenings in nature. Master Usui, the founder of Reiki, received the inspiration for healing and attunements while meditating at the base of a waterfall in Mount Kurama in Japan. It seems, we only have to stop a moment, to rest, and all the insight and answers we are seeking will be ours. Nature and spirituality go hand in hand. We are instantly uplifted by even a moment in Nature.

From Ecologist to Reiki Master — Mother Earth is my Boss!

When I was little, I saw the devastation that existed throughout the world. Even though I was only six, I felt tremendous responsibility to help. I knew I couldn't do it all, so I prayed. I prayed in the way only a six-year-old can, fervently and with great urgency.

"Help me! I can't do it all! I'm only one little girl!"

The answer came almost immediately. "It's okay. Just pick one."

So I did.

I picked one. One issue the world was facing that I felt I could help with. I picked the environment. I would make it my mission to save the natural world, to help in whatever way I could to make the world better. Mother Earth needed me, and I would be there to help her!

I followed through and studied biology, completing a bachelor's degree in zoology and working at the university as a field researcher in ecology. Throughout this time, I fell even more in LOVE with the natural world. The myriad of species that exists on this planet is staggering. I was amazed at all I was learning and how very much more there is to learn.

Even now, we are only just barely beginning to understand how all of these species interact with each other and their environments. The mystery and complexity of life on this planet, this one tiny planet, is still just barely understood.

Alongside the scientific exploration of the natural world I was doing in my studies, I was increasingly drawn to nature-based religions. I could see and feel the planet herself as a Divine Consciousness and the interconnected web of life surrounding her, her woven fabric, draped over her regal shoulders.

A deep reverence for Life in all forms overtook me in my quiet moments. I would get swept away by the wonder of it all and try to comprehend how it could possibly fit all together and how we could possibly understand it. I fell in love with Nature.

I could not understand how people could willfully damage this tremendous gift, Mother Earth.

Throughout my environmental career as a risk assessor, anger fueled my resolve to work on environmental issues, but also burnt me out and nearly made me bitter.

Just at the moment when I was most cynical, I went back to pursue a Master's degree in ecology. If I could just escape the 'real' world for a while and bury my head in academia, I might be able to regain that hopeful and optimistic vision for the future of the planet.

Throughout it all, even from when I was very young, I always saw people as the problem. It was people messing it all up. It took many years before I began to see people also as the solution. People could fix this or, at least, stop causing more harm.

When I began exploring the spirituality of the Earth, I began getting the strong sensation of a consciousness below my feet. A supporting and nurturing presence. There was great wisdom and kindness within these connections to Her energy. I now see the Earth as a strong and resilient entity. The Earth is not some mere, passive recipient of environmental insults. It is a thinking, conscious being.

In a deep meditation a few years ago, I had a vision of Mother Earth merely tolerating our occupation of her surface. If she chose to, she could finish us as a species. One shrug of her shoulder, and we humans would be over. Her experiment in hominids was interesting, but I got this sense she was growing tired of our shenanigans and will give us another 100 years or so to change her mind.

It was a powerful message.

To the Earth, all of life on the planet has occurred in a blink of an eye. There is a vastness to her longevity, and she has seen so many millions of species come and go. Whole families of organisms have come and gone before us. So many more will arise, evolve, and fade after us. One thing is clear, we need her more than she needs us.

We depend entirely on Her for our survival. Mother Earth is far stronger and far more resilient than we even know. It is us who are fragile. It is **us** who we harm when we harm the natural world.

So why would anyone inflict harm on themselves?

Lack of self-love.

This is the answer I keep coming back to. You might argue it is ignorance of the harm that is the problem, but as a whole, I have found most people have a basic understanding of what causes harm to themselves or the planet, but they do it anyway.

I have observed people within industrial companies make decisions that would seem counterintuitive to good common sense, all because they don't want to get into trouble. They avoid taking samples in the best locations, because they don't want to know there is a problem. They are afraid. They are afraid they are bad, and that fear is shame. **Shame** is making these bad decisions. Shame is running the show.

Keep in mind. These are good people. They have families. They volunteer. They even recycle. And yet, many of them consistently make poor choices because of shame. Adding MORE shame to people in big corporations will not solve these big issues. Labeling people as 'bad', just because they work for a big corporation, is not going to get us anywhere. Because 'bad' people can't escape their label, so there is no reason to try changing anything. This is how shame works. It keeps us stuck.

If we want true change, if we want companies to be good citizens and clean up their practices and messes, then we have to lose the 'bad' labels for good.

This is not about dismissing the culpability of corporations and people who have made some terrible choices. These problems exist, and there needs to be action taken. But the words we use are powerful. These are not 'bad' people. These are GOOD people, who have made bad choices. Good people can change their behavior and make better choices. Bad people are stuck. Trapped by a label.

People Are The Solution.

People *are* the solution. They really are! The solution lives within the hearts and minds of the people on this planet. When we change, the world changes. When we are able to care for and love *ourselves*, we are then able to care for and love the planet.

All healing is self-healing. If we want the natural world to heal, then we must begin with ourselves.

Mother Earth is still rooting for us, by the way. Even though we have created giant messes, Mother Earth has not given up on us, yet. We still have a chance. If we are willing to change, we have a chance. She still loves us and wants us to succeed. She is the mother of all Life, after all, and she loves us still.

Meditation

Grounding is a spiritual practice where we consciously connect to the Earth. Grounding is important, because we spend so little time outside in our modern lives. The absolute best way to ground is to actually get outside and put your feet right on the earth. But you can still ground energetically, even if the weather is bad or you are just too busy to go outside.

When people start using grounding in their work and their lives, they are better able to remain anchored in the Divine energy that flows through them. It doesn't matter what kind of work you do, even working in an office, grounding will help you get and stay clear and connected to your Divine inner knowing.

When you connect to the earth for a few moments before work or a big meeting, you feel filled up, rather than depleted. The Divine does the work for you, and you are able to maintain good energetic boundaries between you and the people around you.

With this very simple grounding technique, you will get the same feeling of the support and nourishment you would normally get by being in nature, but it is something you can fit into your busy day. It only takes a few minutes, but it can absolutely change the way you feel and how your approach your life. It gives you a calm and centred feeling and allows you to gain clarity when you have an important decision to make.

I often find that, after spending a few minutes of grounding and breathing, I get immediate clarity on what I need to do. My guidance and intuition are clear, and the mental chatter and chaos is completely silent.

In Reiki, grounding is used before each and every healing session. If you do energy or body work, you will find the practice of grounding in this chapter, and the Divine Light practice you will learn in the next chapter, to be invaluable in preventing fatigue and burnout. Grounding provides balance and stability to healing sessions. It allows any excess or unwanted energy to be safely handled by the wisdom of the Earth.

How to Ground

Grounding is very simple. Keep it simple and serene, just like nature. Use the grounding meditation anytime you feel scattered, off-centre, unbalanced, or feeling unpleasant emotions, like worry, anxiety, fear anger, or rage. You will feel a sense of peace and calm fill you and soothe you.

Just visualize the earth energy and your energy connecting. That is all you need to do.

Try this meditation to guide you deeper into that stable and nurturing connection with the Earth.

Grounding Meditation

Just very gently, as you read this, let your breath relax.

Place your feet flat on the floor and bring your spine up straight.

Just gently, become aware of the energy of the Earth, just below your feet, just below the base of your spine. Notice the vast expanse of energy available to you now. This energy is wise, dependable, and nurturing. Feel the charge and character of this Earth energy now.

Now, become aware of the energy within your body. Observe the difference or similarity between your energy and the Earth's energy.

Just notice this gently, easily, and with great kindness.

Now, easily, with your breath, allow the energy of your body, and the energy of the Earth to balance out. Let the energy reach its own stable resting point, your natural equilibrium.

Allow the charges in your body and in the Earth to harmonize. Just easily and gently, with your breath. Notice how your breath helps the energy flow. Notice the support, the love, the comfort that is available to you now.

There is no need to push or pull the energy here. Just step aside and let it flow.

Allow the Earth energy to rise up your body, right to your crown.

Allow any unwanted energy or tension to flow off, right through your feet.

Let the nurturing presence of Mother Earth be with you now.

Surrender all barriers and blockages to her magnificent love.

You are so loved.

Feel it now.

Rest here for a moment.

When you are ready, wiggle your fingers and your toes. Give yourself a hug, and have a wonderful day!

Sharing Circle

Spend the next 5 minutes writing about your experience in the meditation.

How do you feel now, compared to how you felt before the meditation?

How has your balance improved? Physically? Emotionally? Mentally?

Signs of Spring

Gifts of the Earth

There is no better moment to look for signs of spring than right after grounding.

Take a few minutes to connect to the Earth and write down a quick list of all the ways the Earth helps you on your Journey in Life.

List everything you can think of from your fruits and vegetables at every meal, to the trees and grass outside to your window.

Notice the birds and bugs and mammals that enrich your Divine experience, here on the planet. Notice all the gifts and messages from Nature.

Self Care & Love

Time for another Nature walk!

Go for a walk outside. If you can, spend a few moments barefoot on the earth or sit next to a tree. Maybe even lie down on the ground. Let all your cares and worries be absorbed by the Earth. Allow the Earth to take the toxicity, all of it, and convert it back to fresh, energetic soil, new dirt, new life.

Allow Nature to do what she does best, decompose the old to give space and life to the new. Feel the new energy sprout up within you as you breathe.

Connect to the deep cycles of energy within the Earth. Feel the pulse of Nature beneath your feet. Let this energy sustain you anywhere you might travel, in a car, plan, bus, train, anywhere you might sit, inside at home, at work, at the factory, at the cubicle.

Let Nature follow you there, inside. Let Her fill your days with precious moments of wisdom and clarity. Let her wisdom guide you. Let her love calm you. Feel and know the deep essence of peace within the Earth, so you may, in your own unique way, bring Peace on Earth.

Intuition

Follow your Inner Compass

Deep within the earth, there resides a force. Ancient and timeless, this force has guided humanity in their travels for ages.

The magnetic field within and around the earth guides and protects us, each and every day.

This field is steady. It has not changed for millennia. It surrounds the earth and shields us from damaging particles and ions from the intense radiation of our sun.

The compass is a mystical and magical creation that saves countless lives every year.

You may have heard of the ability of birds and other animals to perform huge migrations, following their inner compass. They can travel huge distances, accurately, using only their own guidance system. These mass migrations are just beginning to be understood. Yet, every year, millions and millions of animals undertake migrations; some even travel pole to pole, transiting the equivalent of the circumference of the earth each year.

As amazing as this may seem, these animals are guided by a deep *pull* within them, an urging they cannot resist. They follow wisdom deep within their cells, their hearts, their minds, and their spirit. That wisdom that lies deep within guides their entire journey.

They may not know the whole route; they may not even be able to understand the journey they are embarking on or the destination. And yet, they go, following that deep call. Following the wisdom within, they make it, without fail, year in and year out. They are following their Dharma, their true soul's path.

YOUR Inner Compass

You too have this deep pull within you. You have your own inner compass. This compass guides you, daily, toward your dreams. It orients you towards what you truly desire and leads you on your own true path, the path of your soul's purpose.

You know this deep pull. You likely have felt it deep within your heart when you made a decision that created expansion in your life. You also probably felt it when you made a choice that created constriction in your life. It is that deep part of us that leaps with joy when we turn toward our purpose and the part that tugs and tugs at us when we turn away from our purpose.

No one else can define or refine this compass for you. Interpreting its messages are your business and no one else's. Sometimes we get confused, frightened, and limited when we follow someone else's compass for too long.

When we allow another to rule our lives, we can neatly excuse ourselves from responsibility for how our lives are turning out. This is victim thinking and never helps you except in the short-term. Excusing yourself from responsibility for your own life does not change the pulse and pull of your inner compass.

Your yearning to follow your Dharma will still be there when the ones you have blamed are gone. You must follow this insistent call of your soul's path. There is no helping it. This is why you came here to this planet!

You may be saying to yourself, "But I don't **know** what my Life Purpose is!! I would follow it if I knew where I was heading!"

Firstly, let go of **thinking** your way there. A migrating bird does not think, "Right. So I go south for 200 miles. Stop at this pond. Turn southwest for another 200 miles and I'm there!"

Nope. They **feel**. They feel their way thousands and thousands of miles to the perfect spot. They **feel** it. And so do you!

You know when you are on your path when you feel increased certainty, joy, and enhanced awareness. You get confirmation of your path when you see an increase in synchronicity in your life. You can't miss. Your luck increases.

You meet the perfect people at the perfect time. You get nudges all along the way.

You also get doors closed in your face. You get endings too. Unhealthy relationships vaporize in the light of you walking your Dharma. When you expand, all unhelpful and unhealthy things drop away.

I am so grateful for all the opportunities that didn't work out. I had several session spaces boot me out and ask me to leave, just as I was expanding into my purpose. At first, it was difficult, because I just wanted to develop a Reiki and reflexology practice. But every time I had a session space fall through, I would turn to writing. Eventually I caught on, I was meant to teach. I started to develop the courses for Reiki, and when I did, it was hugely successful.

All those closed doors taught me I was close, but not quite following the right path for me. My path is curvy, twisty, and twirly. My path is not linear, but it still makes sense. When I am moving in the right direction, everything opens up. It all gets easier. When I am not going in the right direction, no amount of brute force could make things work.

There is *ease* in following the inner compass. And the beautiful thing is, you can never get lost. Even if you used brute force to go in the opposite direction for your whole life, you can find your way again in a matter of minutes. Just breathe, and ground, and listen. Connect into the wisdom and love of Mother Earth, and then ask "What is in my highest and best interest to do, right now?"

Take your first thought as the answer, before the inner negative critic gets a hold of it. This is your direction. You need not see the whole road before you start. It might be something simple, like going to make a sandwich or going for a walk.

It might be something grander, a huge idea or a dream lingering in the shadows your whole life. Whatever guidance you get after you connect to the earth, you can trust it to lead you in the best direction.

You know, always, the best way to go by how it *feels*.

Just for Today — Follow your Compass

Spend one whole day following your inner compass. Do not make any huge decisions or changes on this day. Just make a series of tiny choices of how to best spend the moment, the NOW moment, you are in each and every moment of this day.

Do not trouble the past. Do not fret about the future. Breathe and stay present for a full 24 hours.

Choose a weekend or a day off, so you can be unfettered by your regular commitments.

Follow your sense of ease.

Follow your inner compass and watch what happens!

Affirmations

Try these affirmations to support your connection to the Earth. Read each one and notice how each one feels. Choose the one that zings for you, the one that resonates the most.

Notice how a few moments of affirming your connection to the Earth creates a bigger and more stable energy flow. Notice how you feel. Do you feel calmer? More centered? Secure?

Use these affirmations to consciously connect to the Earth now. Practice these affirmations daily, until they become part of your inner voice.

If you notice any of these affirmations stirring up feelings of anger, worry, criticism, worthlessness, or cruelty, then use the corresponding Reiki Ideal Affirmation Ladder process to ease those feelings before continuing on with the grounding affirmations.

Grounding Affirmations

Grounding into the Earth, I am rooted. I am safe. I am supported.

I trust and follow my internal compass.

The Earth is on my side! Life itself supports me on my journey.

Tuning in and trusting. I am safe within the wisdom of my soul.

Listening to Life buzz and pulse all around and within me, I see the Divine in everything.

Stretching out, down to the earth, up to the sky. I fly. I stand. I smile.

I trust my deep wisdom to support me, always.

I love the Earth and She loves me.

Practice

Your body is the earth of your experience. Your body is the physical emanation of the earth itself, and it houses your spirit for your entire lifetime. What a loss it would be if we got to the end of our days and had to let go of our body, only to realize we never truly loved or appreciated it while we had it.

Bodies are ephemeral. They come and they go through our many lifetimes. We, however, remain. The essence of us, the part of us that makes us truly ourselves is eternal. It goes beyond any one lifetime or physical experience.

Our bodies are the earth of our experience. We work so hard, before we incarnate here, to get the chance to be born on Earth. It is a unique place in all the Universe. Great wisdom and insight can be found here. We can access this even within just one physical lifetime. That is a truly amazing gift, and one not to be squandered. We lose out on all of the spiritual riches this lifetime can hold, when we get obsessed with the way we look on the outside.

So much of the media throughout the world is focused on what we and other people look like, externally, rather than who we are. So much time, energy, and drama surrounds the number on the scale or the one on the back of our jeans. We can completely lose sight of all the ways our bodies are amazing gifts. Our bodies are vessels for life! They house our souls! And anything that does that is inherently precious.

Now, let's be clear. I do not subscribe to the notion we should abandon our bodies for a spiritually devoted life. Far from it! We all worked too hard to get here, in these physical bodies, in the first place!

Bodies are Divine vehicles. They must be tended to and cared for. Your body carries your SOUL! For that alone, it must be honored and praised.

Your body needs fresh water, fresh air, hearty exercise, nourishing food, meditation and prayer, time with friends and family, and time doing blissful activities like sex, creating art, cooking a fine meal, and eating chocolate!

Your body is a gift from the Earth. Every part of your physical body exists because of the food, water, and air you take in and all of those things originate from the Earth. When you take loving care of your body, giving it what it truly needs, you are also taking care of the Earth! The two go hand in hand.

So often, what is best for our bodies is also best for the planet.

Eating whole and wholesome foods, organic and local, is good for the body and is good for the earth.

Walking outside and enjoying nature is good for the body and good for the earth.

Being kind to your body, clothing it lovingly, tending to your hair and teeth and skin and eyes, being gentle with yourself is good for the body and the earth, too!

Time to Ditch the Beauty Ideal and Start Some Body LOVE!

If you tune into mainstream media for any length of time, you are bombarded with hateful propaganda that could teach you, if you let it, that there is only one body type that is beautiful; that all your worth comes from your dress size; that being flawless is the only thing worth striving for; and that no one will love you if you are too fat, too skinny, too white, too dark, too tall, too short, too lumpy, too flat, too curvy, too bumpy, too, too, too, too, too... It never ends.

These external, often profit-driven, beauty ideals are completely fake. There are enough Photoshop before and afters out there to show us that, even people who conform to the beauty ideal still fall short. No one looks like this. No one.

The notion of a beauty ideal is really just a sales gimmick. It is driven by the need to sell lipstick and cars and clothes and diet pills and steroids and 'nutrient supplements'. This beauty ideal is not real, it is fiction. Dangerous fiction.

This fiction falls apart when you start doing self-esteem work and nurturing your spirit. The Divine part within you, as it is given a larger role and voice in your life, will not stand for any abuse. Berating our physical bodies and accepting the cultural shame of not measuring up to these false standards is not compatible with a soulful life.

All your soul sees when it looks at your physical body is love. All the Divine sees when it looks at your body is love. God does not care about your size, shape, colour, or height. Goddess does not care about cellulite, loose abs, or flat chests. The Divine, in all its forms, does not spend a moment withholding love or affection because of how you look. So why do we?

Why spend another moment hating our bodies when the Divine loves us, just as we are? That inner shame and criticism is so damaging to the body. It is just as toxic as if we had swallowed poison.

It is time to stop taking in this cultural poison and shame connected to these false standards. If we stop buying it, they'll stop trying to sell it.

True beauty is always found within

So it is time. Time to let go of an outmoded idea of beauty and replace it with something altogether new.

Here it is: True beauty is generated from within. It is not something you can diet your way into. It is a quality of someone's soul shining out of their eyes when they smile. It is all the tiny acts of service people do to make the world a better place. It is holding open a door. It is asking for help. It is showing emotion and being brave. It is sharing our art, when we would rather hide it away. It is a hug. It is kindness, visible.

Beauty is kindness made visible.

You have beauty. Right NOW. In this moment. The moment you are in, in this exact second. You will KNOW you are beautiful the moment you believe the truth. And here it is:

Everyone's body is a miracle. Your body is a miracle. AND MIRACLES ARE BEAUTIFUL!!

This is true. You are beautiful. Right now! Without changing a hair. You are beautiful. You do not need to lose 10 pounds or 100 to be beautiful. You are beautiful the moment you decide you are!!

That does not sell a lot of creams and lotions and potions. It does not make millions for those who profit off of low self-esteem. But it is true. And you can feel it as truth.

The nice thing is the beauty ideal is only an idea, a thought, and thoughts can be changed.

WE are our culture. If enough of us change our thoughts about what beauty really is, then little girls won't grow up dieting themselves to oblivion, and little boys won't confuse muscles with strength.

We take back our power in the moment we decide to see beauty as an internal quality, rather than an external one.

Life is precious, and it is fleeting. Let's not waste another moment worrying about the flappy skin on our arms and just use those flappy arms to hug someone.

We are beautiful as soon as we stop obsessing over our dimply legs and just splash around the swimming pool with our kids.

We are beautiful as soon as we stop worrying about our big bellies and just work our abs by laughing until we pee a little.

Life is messy. Life is dimply. Life is wrinkles and grey hair and sagging boobs.

I would rather live a long and happy life with a round dimply butt, flappy arms, wrinkles, and white hair all flying around me as I flip-flap my way through my awkward and joyous life than spend another second staring at my supposed flaws in a mirror.

I am the Earth. The Earth is me. You are the Earth. The Earth is you. We take care of the Earth as we take care of ourselves.

Just for Today

Just for today, LOVE the least culturally loveable parts of yourself. Whatever body part has been plaguing you, let it be.

Let it be beautiful in all its awkward flappy glory.

Heap love and abundant kindness on this party of your body. Apologize for saying mean things to it. Apologize for doing mean things to this important part of your body.

Imagine that, just for today, you have the world's most beautiful one. Imagine that the media all shifted overnight, and today your body is the new standard of beauty.

Write in your journal about your experiences as the world's most beautiful person. What have you learned about the nature of physical beauty? What happens to your self-talk when you are not comparing your body to anything else? How do you feel when you need not change anything to be beautiful?

Write an ode to the glories of your beautiful, wrinkly, young, fat, skinny, tall, short body.

Just for today, you are just right.

Sharing Circle

Think of someone you love dearly. Write down how you feel about them. Share with them how much you love them, just as they are.

Now write from the perspective of Divine Love. Write about how loved you are and how amazing you are, just as you are.

Notice how the two writing exercises are similar? How could you add more loving words into the story you tell about yourself?

Stop and Give me 5!

Take a deep breath!

For the next 5 minutes, visualize being surrounded by Nature. Choose a place that renews you. It could be a forest, a meadow, a mountain, a beach, anywhere that makes you feel relaxed.

Travel there now, in your mind.

You are there!

Drink in the beauty with all your senses.

CHAPTER TEN:

Divine Connection

Something opens our wings. Something makes boredom and hurt disappear. Someone fills the cup in front of us: We taste only sacredness.

 ~ Rumi

Divine Energy is Always Available

The Divine loves you.

Yup.

'Tis true.

There is so much love, light, and energy available to you right now. Right in this moment. All the energy you need for everything you need to do is right here for you, just a thought away.

In Reiki, right after grounding, the next step is to breathe in the Divine energy right through the crown, down the spine, and all the way into the belly. This is a visualization practice that immediately connects us to the Divine, our Higher Power, Source, God. We breathe the light right down into our bellies, literally filling up our energy tanks with Divine Light.

This process is done in Reiki, but it really can be used by **anyone** who wants access to Divine energy on a consistent basis.

You can fill up with the Divine Light and receive its wisdom. This technique is a very easy. It only takes a second or two of visualization, and it will completely change your outlook. It is an acknowledgment that the Divine is the ultimate source of all things, and the Divine is **more** than willing to give us what we need. It can be used by anyone to instantly connect to Divine Love and energy.

It is COOL to Ask for Help!

We often get so busy that we forget to ask for help. We forget to pause and breathe and acknowledge the Divine energy available to us. Just with one conscious breath, we can access this eternal and abundant source of love, directly from God and the Universe. With this level of support, we can do anything; we can heal anything; all our dreams are within reach and satisfied at the same moment.

By connecting to the Divine, first, before you do anything, you get the deep feeling of certainty that you are absolutely healthy, whole, and complete. That peace and clarity changes how you hold your body. It settles your shoulders, it relaxes your back, it unwinds your jaw, and opens your palms. You FEEL the trust and faith of the Divine flowing within you.

Everything you do takes less effort when you connect to your Source. Use that divinely-guided energy, not your own personal energy, to accomplish your tasks. Everything will become easy. You will be amazed at how much you can get done when you lean on the arm of the Divine to lead you through. You become more productive with less effort and less stress.

Use Divine Energy to Power your Life

Using your personal energy, as your own source for your daily activities, ends up depleting you. Think of your own energy like a rechargeable battery. If you never plug in, you run out.

Divinely-guided life force energy is infinite, consistently refilling, a limitless supply waiting for you to let it in. It is only waiting for you to access it before it can flow in. When you consciously access this level of energy and bring it into your body, you can accomplish anything, anything at all, that is in your highest good.

You plug into this source with mindful awareness; it is possible to fill up with energy. Just by thinking about the energy flowing in and allowing it to flow to you as strongly as you need it to is all you need to do to begin. When you are filled up, from this Divine Source, you feel vital, peaceful, and clear.

Use the Divine Light Meditation to charge your batteries, whenever you need a boost of energy or inspiration.

Meditation — Divine Light

Take a moment to connect into the flow of energy all around you.

Breathe deeply and tune into the Earth below your feet. Let the energy in the Earth and the energy in your own body balance out. Let it reach its own natural, stable, equilibrium.

Just easily, with your breath, get out of the way and let more energy in. Let the Earth help you now.

Now, gently, turn your awareness to the energy available to you, just above your head. See and feel the Divine Light, waiting for you, just above your crown. Notice the beautiful colour. Notice the pure LOVE, just for you.

Now, breathe this energy in. Through the top of your head, through your crown chakra, all the way through and down to your belly. Let the energy fill up the energetic core of your own body.

Place your hands just below your belly button, right on the energetic and physical center of your body.

With each breath in, the Divine Light flows through your crown and down through your body, and comes to fill and swirl within your belly, right behind your hands.

The energy flows in easily, with zero effort. Just like a waterfall, you need not push it to go faster, you only have to open up and allow.

See if you can let in just a little bit more.

Even more.

Let it all in Now!

Keep breathing in this way, until you are able to feel your energy below your hands fill all the way up. When you are fully charged, your hands will lift easily from your belly. If you need more energy, your hands will feel heavy or comfortable where they are.

You can even visualize a gauge or a dial that fills up, just like the gas tank on your car. Wait until you are at 100% before ending the meditation.

When you are full of Divine Love and Light, lift your hands from your belly. Bring your hands, palms together, in front of your heart.

Reconnect to your body in this present moment. Let any excess energy easily flow off of you, down your legs and back to the earth. Keep the energy you need, resting easily within your belly. Give yourself a hug and a stretch. Your meditation is done.

Have a wonderful day!

Sharing Circle

Spend the next 5 minutes writing about your experience in the meditation.

How do you feel now, compared to how you felt before the meditation?

How does it feel to bring more light into your everyday reality?

Signs of Spring

You are guided and loved and protected in every moment of your life by the Divine. Spend a few minutes now, capturing these little examples of how much you are LOVED by God/ Goddess/ the Divine/ the Universe/ Source Energy.

Self Care & Love

You are amazing, brilliant, blessed, beloved. The Love, deep and eternal, the Universe has for you knows no bounds. You are a magnificent creation of God's Love.

That you exist is all the reason you will ever need to know you are worthy of this immense and condition-free love.

God/ Source/the Divine/the Universe loves you with abandon and without reserve or restriction. It is all there for you. The moment you choose it.

Choose it.

The Divine respects your wishes and boundaries. It cannot help unless you ask!

These Divine Ethics are the same ones followed by the best healers in the world. They wait for the question; they wait for the asking; they listen, and they wait.

The Divine Universe is listening to you, now, and in every moment.

What do you ask for in this moment of LISTENING?

Leave others alone. They can all ask for themselves, and they do in many spoken and unspoken ways. This is about you! Ask for yourself, for your own needs, for your own healing, for you.

Ask and receive.

This is the ultimate self-care, asking for Divine help and then letting it in.

Just for Today — Ask!

Just for today, ask! Ask the Universe to help you with ALL of your activities, everything from carrying in groceries to paying bills and solving problems.

Ask for help with it all.

Nothing is too large or small for the Divine. You can ask and receive help for it all.

Let it in. Let in the answers. Let in the help. Let others (real, physical people) help you. Say thanks and accept the answers to your requests, even if it is not in the way you expected it.

Let the Universe be free. Do not impose limits on how *much* help you are allowed to have. Let the Universe say 'when'. It knows exactly the best way to provide you the help you need at the perfect time you need it.

Accept your good with gratitude, with thanks, with appreciation. Hand over all the details to the Divine.

Stop and Give me 5!

Take 5 short minutes, right now, to bathe yourself in a sea of gratitude and appreciation.

Simmer and savor this feeling. Let it bathe and wash through every cell, every corner of your soul and your mind.

Let gratitude make you bright and shiny. Let it polish you up, so you GLOW with radiance, love, and warmth.

Intuition

Intuition is the process where we raise our energy level to the same frequency as the non-physical beings that guide us, so we can receive their wisdom in a form that makes sense to us.

We make sense of this spiritual information in our third-eye chakra. We put all of the information together in the context of our language, culture, and previous life experiences.

Many people can innately channel messages from the Divine. They seem to be born with this ability. Intuition and the ability to interpret Divine information is something I believe we *all* can do. We can all converse with angels, archangels, ascended masters, Jesus, Master Usui, Buddha, and so many other Divine beings. All it takes is a little belief and a little practice.

You can consciously connect with the energy of these high vibrational beings. You contain a Divine spark within you. You are part of the Divine already, always. It is this part of you that can hear and understand the messages and guidance the Divine has for you. When you truly know and believe in this Divine connection, the natural result is an enhanced awareness and communication with the Divine realm.

If you have a heart and a brain, you can automatically converse with God. There is no other prerequisite needed. Just believing you can get direct messages from Source, with no one else interpreting it for you, is enough.

That belief brings forth the ability to see and hear clearly. The dialogue I have with my Divine Team is amazingly uplifting. I talk to them often, either by a dialogue on paper or by hearing and thinking the response. I open up and let it flow when I write to them.

For me, that has been the easiest way to begin. I set my intention of who I wish to speak to by writing their name at the top of the page. Then I just write.

You can directly access Divine Wisdom. It can be just as simple as asking a question to a trusted friend and receiving your answer. When you go directly to the Source to ask your questions, you get the best, most loving, and wise answers. You know the truth when you hear it. You get a physical reaction in your body, there is an ease and resonance that can give you shivers. It is a deep confirmation that the message is true and accurate and meaningful.

Accurate messages from Source are clear, meaningful, and uplifting. Even when delivering news you would rather not hear, the Divine always leaves you hopeful and with some clarity about your next steps. When you access the Divine, you can get some profound advice to any question on your mind. The advice given lifts you up and gives you your soul's perspective.

Writing to the Divine

Close your eyes for a moment. Take a deep breath and allow the Divine spark within you to speak. If you could choose one Divine Being you trust completely, that you absolutely know has the best intention for you, one Being in whose guidance you know would be completely filled with love, clarity, and support, who would you choose? Who pops into your mind?

Know you can talk to any Divine Being you choose. You can go right to the top of your list. You can talk to God, the Divine Intelligence of the Universe, Jesus, Master Usui, Buddha, Ganesh, Mother Mary, Quan Yin, Abraham, or even your own soul or higher being.

You do not need to work your way up the ladder; you can start talking to the Being that resonates the most with you. The more you love them, the easier it will be to get a clear communication. The Divine dialogue operates at the frequency of love, so the more love you feel, the more you can 'hear'.

Whomever you choose is just right for you. Go with your first response.

Before every Writing to the Divine session, take a moment to get clear. Take a few breaths. Ground, connect to the Earth. Breathe in the Divine Light and fill your belly. Settle into the Divine Love all around you. From this space, you are ready to ask your questions.

Begin by writing the name of the Divine Being you wish to contact at the top of the page. Mark their name and their lines of dialogue with a circle. Write your name at the top of the page and mark your name and lines of dialogue with a dash.

Start your dialogue as you would any conversation. Say hello and thank them for joining you.

Allow the normal conversational response to come through and write it down.

You may ask any question you like, but it is best to start with questions full of integrity. Divine Beings are not interested in talking about why you are unworthy; they just love you and will not listen to you being hard on yourself.

Draw a dash and ask your questions. Draw a circle and write down the first and unedited thing that pops into your mind. Just let the answers flow. You can ask anything you want. These high vibrational Beings *love* questions and *love* talking with you.

Continue as long as you want to and then say thanks for all their help and guidance.

Keep practicing, and soon, you will find you can converse with the Divine Source as easily as talking to a dear friend. The guidance you receive will become clearer and more specific the more you practice. All Divine conversations leave you feeling uplifted and joyful. The guidance given is insightful and very helpful.

As you 'talk' to different Divine Beings, you will find that each one has their own unique voice and style. Some beings have their own areas of expertise, and you can ask them questions about what they are really good at.

Master Usui is my go-to guy for Reiki questions — or anything else really! He is pretty awesome and funny, too! (He says to add that he is also handsome!).

Quan Yin, the goddess of compassion, is amazing to talk to for issues connected to self-care and nurturing. She is also great at seeing the good in anyone and helping with increasing your compassion and kindness for all people. She guards new mothers and babies, and she will help you with issues connected to children and parents (including your own!).

Ganesh, a Hindu deity and the remover of obstacles, will kick your butt if you are wallowing in self-pity or victim thinking. But then, he will also give you a practical plan to dig yourself out of your own mess. He is kind, though, and will only give you things to do that you actually can accomplish. He is GREAT for procrastinating writers! :)

Abraham, the group of beings channeled by Esther Hicks, is amazing at helping you become aware of your vibration. You can learn more about the Law of Attraction and get specific insights into how the universe works and how you can leverage your emotional state to lead the life you wish for.

Jesus is passionately peaceful and joyfully serious. He will help with **anything**. Just ask.

You can talk to passed loved ones on the other side. They are your cheering squad and will help you heal ancestral and old family patterns.

You can also talk directly with the Earth, Sun, Moon, Universe, God. These conversations can be pretty powerful and somewhat surreal, but very, very cool. Just ground appropriately, connecting back into the Earth after a big conversation with BIG energy. It can be a little heady, sometimes, talking to these powerful ones, so just make sure you are fully in your body and back on planet Earth before you operate heavy machinery!

Grounding and visualizing Divine Light filling you is always the best way to start and close a channeling session. It is a nice way to acknowledge you are bringing in this Divine information, so you can better assist the physical world. This is all about you getting practical and meaningful advice, so you can access deeper and more stable contentment and happiness in your life.

It is transformative and life changing work to have these Divine conversations. The wisdom and guidance is so deep, so meaningful, and so practical, that it alone, as a spiritual practice, can transform your whole life.

Affirmations

Try these positive statements and pick one that brings Divine, spiritual energy into your body.

Listen to the tingles!!

That zinging feeling is just one of the sensations the Divine uses to communicate with you. They are confirmation shivers or truth bumps (instead of goose bumps!).

If you notice any of these affirmations stirring up feelings of anger, worry, criticism, worthlessness, or cruelty, then use the corresponding Reiki Ideal Affirmation Ladder process to ease those feelings before continuing with the Divine connection affirmations.

Affirmations for Divine Connection

Divine energy fuels me and fills me now.

I run on Reiki. Divinely-guided life force energy empowers me now.

Divine Love washes over and through me now.

Each moment I breathe, I breathe in Light and Life.

The Divine Loves and protects me for ALL time.

God loves me. I am love.

I am blessed. I love and appreciate my Divinely human existence. All is well.

ALL is well. All is Love. All is Divine.

Divine Energy fills me and is ME. I am THAT.

I AM. Om. I AM. Om. I AM. Om.

Practice

The truest spiritual practice is awareness. Divine energy cannot move or intercede on your behalf, until you stand aside and allow it in.

The Divine operates on the basis of free will. This is the one true gift of a physical, human existence. We get to **choose**. We get ultimate freedom.

The Divine deeply respects this freedom and waits ever so patiently for us to become aware. Awareness brings focus and then choice. A choice to allow all of the Power of God and the Angels to help you, or a choice to struggle on, with all your burdens, alone.

That the Divine gives us this choice at all is an indication of its deep love for us. This is a supremely loving act. Because only in the struggling can one have the thrill of overcoming. To stand atop our mountain of despair and say 'no more', all on our own. It is a fantastic feeling.

The Divine will not rob you of your victories. It will not steal from you these precious moments of testing your mettle, perseverance, and success. The Divine is ever watchful; however, our lifeguard overlooking the pool waiting for the signal we are in trouble and need guidance. Unlike a lifeguard, the Divine will not jump in and rescue you, unless you ask first.

Once you ask, then all manner of help will arrive in weird and wonderful ways. But before this help can arrive, you must be aware of it. This awareness the vast energy and power available to you is most easily activated through meditation.

Just sitting in stillness and having your focal point be the loving presence of the Universe is enough to activate the cosmic flow of assistance you are needing. Divine energy will help you achieve only your highest good and the best result for everyone. Divine energy will not co-operate in destructive or self-destructive behaviour. It will show you the path of compassion, true humility, and love. Only good things result from this kind of deliberate joining up with the Divine.

You are empowered in your ability to heal and grow and help when you bring awareness to the fact that you are not alone.

Just for Today

Just for today, sit in stillness and become **aware**.

Bring stillness to the **presence** of the Divine in your life. You are loved. Be aware of that love.

Allow the Divine Love to show up in your life however it deems fit. Allow it to fulfill the highest and best outcome for all. Let it be free, just as you are free. Acknowledge and be aware of just how much you are loved in this moment, just as you are, right now.

CHAPTER ELEVEN:

Listening

Let us be silent, that we may hear the whispers of the gods.
  ~ Ralph Waldo Emerson

Listening is an Art

Listening is an art. Listening is blossoming and blooming more now, even in our world of chaotic shouting, than it ever has before in our history. This is because the need for listening, **true** listening, has never been greater.

Listening is a treasure in our metaphysical toolbox. We can create magic in our lives by mastering the art of listening.

Listening is like an unexpected $5 bill in a forgotten pocket. It can be surprising just how little is needed to bring joy. The $5 is not a huge amount, but it makes a difference, sometimes a profound difference. Listening is like this. A tiny amount can completely change a situation. Listening is a precious moment when we focus our Divine ability to hear and understand another person. It is a gift.

Listening is easiest when you feel heard by others, but just like compassion, listening becomes a spiritual practice when we bring attention and awareness, to the dialogues that are most difficult. To not reserve our attention and awareness just for our friends or those saying pleasing things, but to also listen to those with opposing or contrasting thoughts and experiences is spirituality in action.

If you want to be listened to, you have to become a good listener first. Not only will you give others a demonstration of your compassion, but you will attract more people who genuinely listen.

Listening **does not** require obedience or a change in your behaviour. You do not need to agree to truly listen. Once you acknowledge your **freedom** to retain your own ideas, you will find listening to be much, much easier. You do not need to blindly accept or follow whatever is spoken. You can separate the act of listening from the act of making choices.

Once you make this distinction, your ability to hear, understand, and acknowledge another viewpoint without it upsetting you skyrockets. You can develop the skill of staying centered in who you truly are and what you truly think and feel about any subject, while acknowledging and respecting another's thoughts and experiences.

True listening allows you to cultivate a centred and stable focus. You develop a 'live and let live' perspective, and you begin to see commonalities where there was once only opposition.

To truly **hear** another is an act of compassion. You need not follow or agree or condone what is said in order to listen. You only need to be patient and create space and time for the person to express themselves. Waiting until they are done speaking, asking questions, looking at them, turning off distractions all indicate your focus and attention. When you allow the other person this space, they become calmer and actually speak less because they know there is no need to repeat themselves.

Side note: Listening is about Kindness, NOT tolerating abuse

Of course, abuse is not to be tolerated. You do **not** need to accept abuse in any form, at any time, from anyone. Period. Full stop.

If you are in an abusive situation, leave. Get help and leave. Sometimes, listening is **not** required. Abuse is one of those times.

Even in abusive situations, however, we can put our power of listening to work to protect ourselves. True listening can keep us safer in troubled times by helping us notice a gap or break in routine that will enable a safe exit from the situation.

Get help to leave safely. Leaving an abuser is the most dangerous moment for a survivor. If you are being abused, reach out and get help from a support agency in your area. There are police, therapists, councillors, and shelters out there to support and protect you. Make a plan and go carefully.

You do not need to accept unloving, unkind, or hurtful words or behaviour. Love yourself and get out.

Leaving an abuser might feel like jumping across a chasm. There is the unknown. There is uncertainty. There is the void. What every person in the midst of abuse needs to know is that, while you are only able to see the blackness and void of the chasm, people in support agencies can see the bridge out.

They can see the danger, but also the resources that will help lift you up and out of the darkness. They know it is a big jump, so they put down safety nets and ropes and pulleys and ladders to help you move to safety. They will help ease you out of the darkness with grace and light. They will help you rebuild your dignity and self-love. They care. They want to help. They will listen.

Love, support, and healing await you. It will be okay.

Listening is Valuable

When you are with someone who truly listens, you feel valued, special, and appreciated. You can give that gift to someone else, when you listen deeply.

Listening is more than just shutting up while the other person talks. Listening is not thinking about what you want to say while the other is speaking. Listening is about giving your full and undivided – *put your cell phone down please* – attention – *look in my eyes please* – to – *turn your body towards mine please* – what it is you – *lean in a little please* – are doing, just listening.

We all know when we are being listened to. We all know when we are not.

The benefit of listening with your full attention is that conversations get **shorter**, not longer. Conversations get more meaningful, not less, when we momentarily surrender our urge to shout the other person down, or assert our opinion, or proceed to rescue, help, or intervene in the conversation.

Listening teaches us to value the other person and when we do, we in turn teach them to value us.

You receive what you give in a conversation. If you are feeling unheard, it is time to really listen. If you listen closely, you will be able to find the people who will make you feel heard and loved and respected.

Attention is Good Listening Behaviour

Attention is powerful. It is one true gift you can give another person. Nearly everyone craves attention and doesn't get enough of it. Simple things, like looking in someone's eyes when they are talking, responding to their speech, turning your body to face them, leaning slightly toward them, ignoring distractions, these tiny behaviours are all signals to the person that they matter, they are important, and you value them.

Please note that listening is different from the physical act of hearing. If you have trouble hearing or you have no hearing, you can still listen. Listening is about attention and focus, not hearing.

Being attentive is more than just showing up and being in the same room. It is focus and understanding. It is a pure expression of compassion and empathy. It is also more than listening to a person's surface words; it is listening to their needs, to what they are trying to express. It is listening to what their heart is trying to communicate. Heart Listening.

Meditation

Meditation hones our ability to listen. It allows us the space to find comfort in an otherwise uncomfortable situation. It allows us to find stillness in the midst of chaos.

The practice of meditation allows us that rare ability to see all sides of an issue without needing to agree or disagree, act or not act. Either way, we can remain impassive in our still center, while others can remain free to think and feel however they choose.

This act of separation, of listening from agreement, is powerful and freeing. Conflict, especially internal conflict, disappears when we gain the *power* of listening with our full attention.

Follow this short, mindful meditation to increase and enhance your listening muscles.

Listening Meditation

Breathe in.

Breathe out.

Feel your feet upon the floor – your bottom against the chair – your head stacked neatly over your shoulders, your shoulders over your hips.

Let the breath travel over you from head to foot in one smooth wave.

Take ten delicious breaths in this way.

Let the wave of your breath wash over you from head to foot, head to foot, head to foot.

Slowly.

Easily.

Gently.

Good.

Now bring your awareness to the power of listening.

Become aware of all the sounds in your environment.

Notice the high sounds. Maybe a bird is singing somewhere; maybe some children are laughing. Listen now for the high sounds.

Notice all you can. Focus on each sound as it comes and goes. Leaving you, still, rooted, in the present.

Sound occurs only in the NOW moment. When you focus, when you listen, all sounds are happening NOW.

Noticing sounds as they occur can only happen in present moment awareness. You are present. You are NOW.

Notice now, the low sounds. Maybe it is the rumble of a bus; maybe it is the voice of the wind; maybe it is the low beat of your own heart. Listen now to the low sounds.

Notice all you can.

Now, notice the low sounds and the high sounds together.

Notice all the sounds between them.

If there is a disturbing sound, see if you can hear other sounds around it. Notice how your awareness and focus makes even quiet sounds more prominent, more noticeable.

It is not the volume that matters here, It Is your awareness. The intensity of your awareness is what matters.

Listen with your WHOLE attention.

Listen with your WHOLE body.

From head to foot, head to foot, head to foot, LISTEN.

Wash yourself in the wave of listening. BE Listening. Become the Listener, the Divine Listener.

Then, when you are ready, wiggle your fingers and toes.

Stretch up – Gently.

Rub the palms of your hands together generate some heat.

Gently cover your eyes with the palms of your hands.

Gently cover your ears.

Bring your hands together in front of your heart.

Bow to your Inner Listener.

Namaste.

Sharing Circle

Write down what you heard.

Listen with the ears of love as you tell your story.

Allow others the gift of listening to you.

Self Care & Love

Listening is, ultimately, an act of self-care. It is a spiritual practice that will net you tremendous personal benefit, especially when you separate the act of listening from any movement within your being.

You need not move from your position. You need not move your thoughts. You need not take action. You need not change your emotions. You do not need to do any of these things to listen fully. You only need to be present, engaged, and aware.

Listening is required for a spiritually fulfilled existence. Listening trains you in present moment awareness. Being present and engaged and aware is made easier when the focus is another's words. That focus can stay with you long after the conversation is over.

When your mind enters the present, you are instantly powerful. It is only in the present moment we can make decisions, set our intention, and direct our focus. When we do these things, we manifest whatever is needed or wanted in our lives.

It is also a huge act of self-care to be listened *to*. Having someone close to you, who will listen to your thoughts and dreams and wild imaginings is a precious gift. As you do this self-development work, you may find your circle of friends shifting to allow more space for true listeners.

This shift in friendships is perfectly normal and natural. When people in your life are on a different vibrational trip than you, sometimes the result is walking down different roads. You may find this has created a gap or two in your circle of friends. Maybe it feels more like a drifting apart; that is also okay. This temporary void will quickly be filled by those who will return the fine, high quality friendship and companionship you can offer.

One-sided relationships where all you do is bleed your energy, time, and resources out on one who hardly ever returns the favor cannot exist in the realm of self-love you are now feeling.

Be assured; new and amazing relationships are on their way to you. Surely and steadily, these amazing friends are on their own journey. Your paths are about to cross. Let go of the 'how' of it all. These amazing people exist. And they are also looking for you!

Amazing people are everywhere! They really are. I have met many of them, and I keep meeting more every day. Soon, if not already, you will too.

The Universe conspires on your behalf. You will meet these kindred souls, these Divine Listeners, in wild and wonderful ways. Just keep doing your work. Just keep meditating, doing affirmations, and following your own joyous heart. You will be led to many amazing friends. They will enter your experience at the perfect moment. The perfect time and place is all being orchestrated for you.

Just for Today

Just for today, call up the person, who has offered the best example of listening you have experienced. This could be a friend, a colleague, a family member, or a mentor.

Great listeners may not talk all that much, but when they do, they have the most fascinating things to say. Wisdom is found in the Listener's mind.

Invite this great listener to a coffee or tea, your treat, and ask them these questions:

1. *What is your idea of a perfect day?*
2. *What do most people get wrong about you?*
3. *Name three things that always make you laugh.*
4. *If you could only take one of these to a deserted island, which would you pick: a book, a music player, a guitar, or a pen and paper?*

5. *What is your favorite season and why?*

6. *If you ruled the world for a day, what would you do?*

7. *What is your favorite memory?*

8. *Congratulations! You just won $5 billion. Now what do you do?*

9. *An alien comes to Earth and asks you to tell them about the best and most beautiful parts of living on Earth. What do you tell them?*

10. *What makes your heart sing?*

11. *What are you most grateful for?*

12. *What inspires you?*

Some of these questions are serious; some are not. The main thing is to get your listener talking. Use these to get the ball rolling and then ask your own questions. Be curious and open minded. Be a good listener to the ones that listen to you! As you listen, you will learn more about what listening can really mean. It is the doorway to wisdom.

Intuition

Intuition is largely about listening. Both are receptive practices. Both are yin, feminine activities that require openness and an attitude of acceptance and compassion.

While acting on and speaking about your intuitive messages is masculine in energy, the actual act of intuition is receptive and feminine in its energy. Do not confuse receptive with passive, however. All intuition is guidance coming to you from high vibrational frequencies. Intuition requires your willingness, involvement, and interpretation.

Just like a radio receiver, you essentially have to put up your antennae and tune in the dial to clearly receive and understand the messages you get. Otherwise it is just static, just noise.

What we want is clear and concise signals that are easy to understand. Messages from the Divine are in our collective best interest. We set our dial to the highest frequency, and then we can receive the best messages. We call upon the Divine, the Divine speaks, and we listen.

Try the following practice to expand your connection with the Divine and to boost the clarity of your intuition.

Just for Today — Listen to the Divine

Just for today, practice listening to the Divine.

First, sit up straight and take a deep breath.

There! You just tuned up!

Breathing consciously and with awareness shifts your energy signature, so you can receive clear signals from the Divine. You essentially put yourself on the Divine wavelength when you breathe fully and deeply.

As you breathe, become aware of your entire body. Your whole body is one big antennae for Divine signals.

Check in with your body now.

What are you feeling? Are there areas of expansion or restriction? How do your hands and feet feel?

Buzzing, warmth, tingling, and surreal kinesthetic experiences, like your hands feeling two sizes too big, are indicators of connecting to the Divine energies. You are tuning into higher, non-local frequencies; you might experience them in many different ways. Whichever way *you* feel it is just right for you.

You are receiving millions of bits of sensory data every second from many different sources all at once. Much of this data is ignored by your brain, so you can make sense of the world around you and not get overwhelmed. When you breathe consciously and deliberately and turn your focus to the Divine signals all around you, you enhance your ability to receive and interpret this information.

You will become increasingly aware of the many ways the Divine can communicate with you as you consciously turn your focus to the Divine. It isn't always a singing and dancing light show. It isn't always hearing or seeing spirit through clairvoyance or clairaudience. Often, it is a feeling, a knowing, a subtle tug in one direction or another, a peaceful connection and sense of calm. It is an internal signal within the core of your being that is unmistakable.

Begin to think of your whole body as one giant *ear* that *listens*.

Just spend time listening to the Divine. Listen to the Universe. Listen to the beat and rhythm of Nature. Listen to the stars twinkling. Listen to the moon. Listen to the trees and grass and flowers. Listen to the birds. Listen to the **Voice** beyond the voice.

Listen.

Affirmations

Listen to yourself speak each of these affirmations out loud. Choose the one that sounds the best.

If you notice any of these affirmations stirring up feelings of anger, worry, criticism, worthlessness, or cruelty, then use the corresponding Reiki Ideal Affirmation Ladder process to ease those feelings before continuing on with the Listening affirmations.

Affirmations for Listening

I listen.

I am a good Listener.

I use Divine guidance to know when to speak and when to listen.

When I choose to speak, I am always heard by God/the Divine/the Universe.

The Universe Listens to me. I choose my words wisely and with great love.

The Microphone is always on. I am heard.

I receive Divine Messages for the best and highest good of all.

Stop and Give me 5!

Set a timer. For the next 5 minutes, just LISTEN.

Deeply listen. Notice all the sounds. Be grateful for all you hear from the Inner and outer ear.

Practice

Deep Listening is connected to the Buddhist practice of Deep Looking. Deep Looking is where you observe the Buddha nature in every being you meet. You deliberately turn your attention to the Divine spark, alive and well, within every being you meet. The more you look for it, the more you see it.

It is the same with Deep Listening! You listen for the Divine essence of what you are hearing. You listen, not just to the voice of the person talking, but also to the Divine spark within them. You listen deeply to their Divine aspect, yearning to communicate with you.

Sometimes, Deep Listening is difficult if the person's words do not match this deeper communication. That is why I love this listening practice: Begin Deep Listening by listening to living beings that make **no sound**.

I like listening to plants and trees for this practice. They are alive, wise, but impassive and not so talkative! Trees will not bore you with idle chatter about the weather or other surficial topics. Trees will not say one thing and do another. Trees are internally and externally consistent.

Trees are also the best listeners, so their wisdom is profound and eternal. Many types of trees live longer than humans. It is a deep joy to listen to these old ones.

Because you are listening to the Divine within these trees, which makes no physically audible sound, it is great practice for when you are listening to the inaudible dialogue within a more talkative being, like a human. You use the same method of listening, no matter if it is a tree or not!

Now, this practice is more about the process, refining your ability to witness, observe, and become aware of deeper energies within the natural world. The results are not as important as being willing to listen to something that has no obvious means of communication. As you experiment with listening to trees you gain the practice needed to listen to more complex life forms! Plus, it is fun! Play along. :)

I have found that each tree has its own character and personality. Some of the younger ones are glib and playful. Some older ones are serious and not all that interested in us weird humans. Be patient. It takes some time for the trees to open up and speak. They won't speak until you are fully engaged and conscious. Be patient. Sit still. Listen.

You can also connect to the essence of a tree by inhaling their essential oil. As you breathe deeply, you can turn your attention to the spirit of the tree. Get still and listen.

Deep Listening is for Humans too!

Once you have practiced Deep Listening for trees, you can expand this practice to people! Take the same patience and awareness you used to listen to the trees and apply it to people.

People are unsure if you really care. They are waiting to be heard. They also are waiting until they have your *full* attention before they will share anything meaningful with you.

As you begin to Deep Listen to people, you will find a shift in the types of conversations you have. People will begin to open up and share more of themselves with you. They will share their hopes and dreams and vulnerabilities. They will share their wisdom and their stories.

This type of deeper and more meaningful conversation is supported by Deep Listening. It creates lasting connections between people. And connection so important to well-being.

You are better able to understand the other person, and you are able to hear their deep request for love, empathy, and understanding.

Just for today, practice Deep Listening.

Signs of Spring

Can you hear that?

Notice how pausing and listening has opened up possibilities in your life. Spend a moment now in gratitude and appreciation for all the myriad ways you are heard. Be grateful for your ability to Listen Deeply.

CHAPTER TWELVE:

Patience

To the mind that is still, the whole universe surrenders.
  ~ Lao Tzu

The Waiting Room

So, here we are. Just waiting around – again – for something to happen, someone to show up, for the show to start, for dinner to be ready, to get onto the next thing, and the next thing, and the next thing, and the thing after that.

Oh! Wait!

Now we are dead!
Where did the time go?

Ok, so patience is lame, right!? Patience is something pathetic people have for important people, right!? Patience is for everyone else, not me, right!?
Um...

Well, by now, you know how I am going to answer that one!

Patience is about surrendering to the present moment. It is not about struggling against the flow of time. It is about embracing the current of life and riding it out in trust and faith.

It is the ultimate test to see if you have mastered present moment awareness. The need for patience often arises when we need it most. It tests your ability to find ease in the midst of uneasiness and vulnerability.

Patience is only hard when we cling to events unfolding in a particular way. When we accept and acknowledge the moment for what it actually is, patience comes easy. All we need is to embrace the NOW, just now, that is all, just this moment, and the next one.

Patience arises when we leave behind the thought that **we** know how everything is **supposed to** turn out. When we stop dictating that circumstances must always please us, then those same uncomfortable moments no longer bother us.

It requires us to ease up. To loosen up. We have to let go of control and trust. Really, patience occurs when we finally surrender the illusion we know better than the Divine.

Patience is only difficult when we are uncomfortable. When we are sitting in our emotional, mucky, 'stuff' — that emotional and vulnerable stuff — we lose patience very quickly. As you work through your vulnerability and recognize the gifts of being courageous, patience becomes possible. Sitting still and not running from the uncomfortable moment shows us how far we have traveled through and out of our messy muck!

Patience is elevated to a spiritual practice when we no longer struggle against the moment, but acknowledge and accept it. There is no numbing. No avoiding. No running away from the awkwardness. Just awareness and presence to the NOW.

Patience is learned. It requires practice. Only when your patience is tested are you able to expand your ability to be still and wait.

Waiting need not be a passive process. Just as with listening, waiting is about being fully engaged and present within the current moment, not one before or one after, but this one, right now.

When you are fully present, waiting disappears. Life is not waiting. It happens real time. Every moment you spend waiting for the next thing to happen, you are not fully aware of what *is* happening now. And *now* is when life is lived!

The urge to avoid the present moment appears most strongly when we are dealing with our emotional muck. So watch for feelings of boredom as really an avoidance tactic to scoot away from vulnerability. Don't numb boredom. Persevere through it and know it is just trying to cover up a vulnerable feeling. Deal with the feeling and boredom fades.

Stop and Give me 5!

Well… it is the patience chapter! So, stop and give me 15!

Yes. Fifteen. One-Five.

Sit. Breathe.

That's it.

No scratching. No shifting. No talking.

No moving at all.

Be still. 15 minutes. You can do it!

Meditation

When you have to be patient, you are being given an opportunity to meditate.

Mindfulness is a meditation technique that allows you to let your experience be as it is, without making a move to change it. It is focusing on the present moment that frees you from the attachment to things being a certain way. Mindfulness is a doorway to happiness. It is training to have a peaceful and calm mind, no matter what is happening externally.

The curious thing is, as soon as you lean in towards acceptance of what is bothersome, it no longer bothers you (or at least, not nearly as much as it did before).

Meditation and patience seem almost impossible when we are faced with pain. Whether the pain is emotional or physical does not matter. Pain is the ultimate distraction from the present moment. We seek to escape the present moment the most when we are faced with severe pain. Even the thought of future pain is enough to send us to numbing behaviours or medications (legal or not).

While being present-minded when we are in pain is difficult, it is often the easiest and fastest ways to relieve the pain we feel. Instead of running away from the uncomfortable or painful moment, we dive into it. We fully acknowledge it and just make space for it to be. It is there anyway. Denying the pain, emotional or physical, just doesn't work. It is there.

I learned of the power of mindfulness to manage pain when I started to experience migraines. I quickly discovered the pain would ease or subside completely if I focused on the core of the pain. I would keep my awareness on the center of where my head hurt the most, almost chasing it down as it would shift.

As my awareness would shift, so would the pain. The pain itself would lessen, and I would feel the migraine subside or disappear altogether. Denying the pain wouldn't help. In fact, it made it harder to manage later. The more present I was, the better I would feel.

This power of mindfulness to conquer pain cannot be understated. Most pain can be managed or reduced by mindfulness. And that is not just my experience talking! More and more data[6] has shown the power of mindfulness to reduce many physical and emotional symptoms. As the research progresses, we are getting scientific confirmation of what the monks have known all along; meditation works! Meditation brings peace, contentment, and lasting happiness.

In the following meditation, I teach you the technique I use to manage pain in body, mind, or emotions. When you are able to manage the pain that is underlying impatience, you are better able to be present to the current moment. I personally use this meditation to manage migraines as well as deep emotional pain, like grief and loss. It has helped me so much I want to share it with you.

Mindful Meditation for Pain Relief

This meditation will help you relieve pain. The pain could be in your body, mind, heart, or soul.

When we have trouble being patient, there is some underlying discomfort. That discomfort is pain, plain and simple. You cannot run from the moment that is uncomfortable. You cannot run from the pain. Instead, choose the opposite. Run toward the pain and see what happens.

---

[6] There are over 3,000 peer-reviewed articles on PubMed, a medical literature database, on the effectiveness of meditation.

Take a deep breath, now.

Close your eyes and gently scan your body, mind, and emotions.

Fully acknowledge your pain levels now.

Stop running and be still. Acknowledge it. Name it. Invite your pain to sit with you.

Stop fighting.

Stop hiding.

Just for a moment, be still.

Breathe deeply.

Now, go further. Follow the pain. Go deeper. Travel towards the centre of the pain. Go right to the heart of it. Go to where it hurts the most.

Not provoking it. Not to fight it. Just to see where it is. Just to see where it lives. Just to listen.

Where is it?

In your body? In your mind? In your soul? In your emotions?

Wherever it is the most acute, go there, now, with your focus and attention.

Travel there.

Dive in deeper.

If it moves, follow it to where it is the most prominent. Follow it to where it moves. Don't let it get away from you.

Be present with the pain. As it shifts, moves, intensifies, or decreases, follow it. Stay with it. Dance with it.

All the while, acknowledging it.

Notice that the pain is not constant.

It ebbs and flows.

It moves.

It shifts.

Pain moves through your experience, just as clouds move across the sky.

The sky is not the clouds; it is something more.

I he sky is there, always observing.

Be like the sky, now. Be here. Observe. Be present.

Breathe.

Scan your body, mind, emotions, and soul. How has the pain changed?

Maybe it is gone. If it is gone, let it go. Let it be gone.

If it is still there, that is okay too. All in good time. The pain will ease, and things will change.

Observe the shifting, changing, flickering nature of pain. Change is in its nature. It is in its nature to diminish, once the signal has been heard and acknowledged. Allow the pain space to be, just as it is.

Observe whatever is happening within your body-mind and spirit. Right now.

No need to run anymore.   You can take a deep breath.

No need to hide anymore.   Breathe deeply.

No need to fight anymore.   Soften.

These clouds will shift and move on too. It is the nature of clouds to change, to be impermanent. So too is your pain. It is impermanent.

Acknowledge this new reality.

Let it ease. Let pain do what it is supposed to do, alert you to a problem. Acknowledge it and let it move on.

Let it go.

Let it be.

You are free.

Spend a few moments, now, breathing deeply into the center of your experience. Acknowledging it. Observing it. Letting it change. Letting it go. Letting it be.

Gently wiggle your fingers and toes. Take another deep breath, and give yourself a hug and a stretch. Your meditation is done.

Sharing Circle

Spend the next 5 minutes writing about your experience in the meditation.

How do you feel now, compared to how you felt before the meditation?

How might meditation help you move through difficult times?

Self Care & Love

Taking time for yourself to do something enjoyable, soul-nurturing, fun, or playful is rare in our often hectic, busy, and fast-paced lives. If you are anything like me, you have a packed-full calendar with double bookings and multiple priorities to balance. Getting the time and space to spend on yourself and ONLY yourself is often seen as indulgent or unproductive.

But nothing could be further from the truth!

How can you possibly expect to properly care and nurture others if you don't take care of yourself!?

It has never been more important to take time to stop, rest, play, and basically enjoy the life we are all working so hard to create. The world needs its caregivers. But if we all collapse from exhaustion and burn out, we are not going to do anyone any good.

Precious Nothing

This self-care exercise is vitally important, and it could be the hardest one yet!

Get out your calendar. Yes. Right now.

Book an entire hour for you. Just you. To do... **NOTHING.**

Yup. That is right.

Book it right now. We all know if it doesn't land in your calendar, it won't get done.

You are taking a non-doing approach here. You are not using your Nothing Time to do laundry, or chores, or to take care of tasks on your To-Do lists. It is time off. Time to goof off and do nothing.

Time. All your own.

Get a babysitter. Turn off your phone (Yup. Right OFF!). Don't answer emails. Don't surf Facebook or social media. Don't spend it on anyone else. Don't do anything productive.

For one hour, this is your precious Nothing Time. It is not booked up with anything. But it is definitely booked!

It is time for puttering, for playing, for sipping a coffee or tea, for watching flowers grow, or for listening to the wind rustle the leaves, or to watch the snow sift down and drift. It is time for daydreaming and doodling and singing songs you just made up. It is time for strolling and sauntering and lolling and loitering.

Get a good loiter in!

This is Precious Nothing!

Walk into a store. Saunter around. Peruse all the racks. Walk out.

Please, please, please. Do nothing during your Precious Nothing hour!

Gift yourself this hour, at least once a week. You will be amazed at how much your life will expand, get more creative, more productive, and more enjoyable, just with one hour, one purely self-indulgent hour, a week.

Signs of Spring

Imagine a garden, where all your thoughts are plants.

Weed out the unwanted ones.

Water the beautiful ones.

Make a list of all the beautiful ones.

Intuition

Patience and intuition go hand in hand. You accurately receive when you are able to set aside the time and mental space to make room for a Divine conversation. When you sit still and wait, with the expectation of receiving, the Divine shows up, is present, and your intuition and clarity expand.

Patience is the same attitude that the Divine has for us. So when we are patient, when we adopt an attitude that matches the Divine, we are putting ourselves on the same vibrational frequency as God, the Angels, and the Universe.

The Divine patiently waits for us to ask for help. The Divine waits and listens. It waits for the question, before it can give an answer. The Divine is the best teacher of patience. Living by example. Waiting for us.

Sometimes when we get impatient, we forget we have the Divine as an ally. Delay, obstacles, and frustrations seem to be the opposite of a kind and loving Universe. When we feel thwarted, we might feel like there is a punishing aspect of the Divine or we haven't yet paid all our Karmic dues. But, always, the Divine *is* on our side.

There is a tremendous power in reversing this thought and instead acknowledging that waiting, delaying, and overcoming obstacles is actually to our **benefit**. It is the result of a kind and loving Universe.

When we consider everything that occurs in our experience is actually the Universe communicating with us, we gain a whole new level of understanding and a whole new level of healing.

This **is** a loving Universe. You are not being blocked; you are being helped.

Just for Today — Acknowledge the Benefits of Delays

Just for today, examine the blocks in your path. Any delay or resistance you encounter, even waiting a bit longer at the grocery store, is a gift from the Divine. Open up and be willing to interpret these messages as your highest good manifesting.

There is something to learn here. What is it?

There is something to know here. What is it?

There is a gift hidden here. Where is it?

Look around and see the messages the moment of delay has for you. Notice the love of the Universe in this pause.

Affirmations

Use affirmations to boost your ability to be patient with yourself and others. Take your time here. No need to rush. Try out each of these affirmations twenty times before choosing one.

Spend the time to savor each one and feel how each is a different flavor.

Then, pick your favorite.

If you notice any of these affirmations stirring up feelings of anger, worry, criticism, worthlessness, or cruelty, then use the corresponding Reiki Ideal Affirmation Ladder process to ease those feelings before continuing on with the patience affirmations.

Patience Affirmations

There is more than enough time.

As I wait, the perfect moment is unfolding before me.

I accept this gift of mindful practice.

I am still. I am here. I am now.

All things arrive at the perfect moment, including me.

I am calm. I am peaceful. I am serene.

I am still within this single Divine moment. All time is mine.

I capture moments as I embrace life.

I am easy and relaxed. All good is for me.

All is in perfect order. All is well.

Practice

Patience is a practice that lasts a lifetime, but it is only lived in a moment. This is what life is about — moments.

Surrendering the ego's agenda, letting the Divine guide you, allowing your life to get really, really good, leaning into the tender, yet blissful moments — these are the gifts of a patience practice.

This entire book is dedicated to happiness, to joy, to peacefulness, and to love. How truly blissful it is to rest in the single now moment you are living! To only absorb and measure our lives by what is occurring in this single beat of our hearts. Divine!!

Letting go of anger and worry, embracing gratitude, the work, and kindness are simple things.

They bring us step by step to the Door of the Divine. And when we open that door, what we see inside is ourselves. It is just us.

We are Divine. *We* are the peace and joy we are seeking.

That joy and happiness is in us. It has been there all along. The practice of patience does not end when you close this book. The work and transformation you have created does not stop. The Universe itself will offer you moments that must be persevered, moments to surrender to, for that is all that can be reasonably done.

This practice of patience is really about embracing life, embracing our vulnerability, embracing our fear and folly. No more running from the life we are actually living. Right this moment — this is your life — right now. The only way it gets better is to start loving the heck out of it.

Instead of running or wishing for something other than what we have got right now, allow the moment to unfold. Allow what is not needed to be released and what is needed to enter. See if you can just scootch over a little bit and make some more room for good in your life.

Can you let in more? Can you actually accept all the good on its way to you in this moment?

It is okay if you are not quite ready. It is okay if you are only letting in 80%. It is okay if you are only letting in 2%. You are letting something in, and that is a brilliant start.

The practice of patience I will leave you with is not patience for others, not for a situation, nor for anything else. The practice is to be patient with *yourself*.

Just for Today — Gift yourself some Patience

Just for today, be patient with YOU. Be gentle with YOU. As you navigate your own twisty, turny, not even a bit linear life, be patient with yourself.

You are a piece of the Divine.

Be kind and loving with yourself. Gift yourself some patience. You are doing so very well, and I am so **very** proud of you!

The Divine Light in me bows to the Divine Light in you. Namaste.

BONUS CHAPTER!

Master Usui's Chapter!

Channelled with love from Master Usui!

Well. Here we all are. At the end.

Let me tell you, the concept of ending is false. There is no ending to life. There is only beginnings and possibilities.

Everything you surrender on the death of your physical body is false. Everything you take with you — your love, your experiences, your kindness and gratitude — that is all **real**. It persists. It lives on as you do.

You survive what you call death. You carry on and sit at the table with all those ones you admire. Jesus, Angels, Mary, Buddha, Lao Tzu, all of the ones who watched over your physical existence. You sit with them and reminisce.

They are all so eager to learn from *you*.

That is the gift of the physical human lifetime. There are learnings that can only occur on Earth. There are unique experiences of separation, loss, and despair.

These are unfathomable to us on the other side. It is like trying to remember a bad dream in the bright light of midday. It vaporizes. For us, living in Source, it is impossible to be separate from the Universal Life Force often called God. We are in it all the time.

When you live in a state of constant connection and communion, it is difficult to understand separation from the Divine. It is like separating a fish from the sea; when the fish is in the ocean, the concept of the air is a philosophical one, not anything experienced. It is a foreign concept, but a fascinating one.

What we know, but you have forgotten, is just how much a part of the Divine you actually are.

You are.

You are inextricably linked to the Divine, because you are made of Divine material. Even your atoms are physically coalesced energy. Even they know their Dharma, that path in the light. Your atoms have never forgotten that they belong to the WHOLE.

Maybe spend some time looking there, in your atoms. If you are so infatuated with the idea that matter is the only truth of your experience, spend some time gazing into your atoms. Spend enough time looking inside the atom, and you will begin to see yourself staring right back!

Spend enough time gazing in to the eyes of a newborn child or a beloved pet and you will also see yourself, then God, then your child or pet, then you, then God.

It is all linked within its separateness.

You are separate, in some aspects, but only so much as to have the freedom of movement and of choice.

This choice is crucial. This choice is beautiful. Your ability to choose and focus, choose and focus, choose and focus – *that* is what really gets the world spinning. That is what causes tremendous expansion and manifestation.

You have a part to play in the Universe. Your decisions matter. Your decisions *affect* matter. You impact the Universe far more than you realize. It is all connected. It is all interconnected.

At the moment of decision, a choice, you set profound energies to work. There are all of us, helpful spirits, sure. But there are also the energies of stars, of atoms, the Whole Universe. It all responds to your choice. The wave of some of your decisions echo all the way through time.

You matter.

You are needed.

Every time you are disciplined in your work, your true spiritual work, you positively affect the Whole in ways you will only understand when you are sitting around the table with us at the end of your physical life. You would have to let go of your 3D thinking and concept of time to fully understand it all.

But for now, the most important thing for you to know is that you matter. You are important to us. You are important to the Universe. We learn when you do, not before. We have access to a higher perspective, not being restricted by bodies or the slowness of your world, but the ability to create, choose, decide, focus, intend — these are all aspects of your Earth. These things do happen on the other side as well, but slower. Much slower. We are not as motivated by the illusion of death, so naturally, less creation comes forth.

Your curiosity and interest fuels much energy. That energy gives form to the solution to every problem, immediately. Then we work with you to help you receive your answers. But it always begins with you.

You live in a beautiful time. Thoughts can manifest in days if you are ready. Plus, you do have the slowness of time on your side too! Negative thoughts take more time to manifest and do not create negative consequences nearly as fast as positive thoughts.

This is because the underlying vibration of the Universe is the frequency of LOVE. The closer you are to this blissful and expanded state, the easier and faster everything lines up for you.

The challenge of your physical world is to balance the enjoyment of it with the truth of its impermanence. It does not last, and it does not stay the same. Enjoy the world. Enjoy your body. Enjoy your abundance and beautiful things. Just don't make physical objects the primary focus of your life.

Physical objects are impermanent. Clinging to them will only bring pain. Enjoy them, just don't get captivated by them. Savor the beautiful things, but remember you only take the joy with you, only your experience transcends your physical form. Make joyful experiences.

Focus on joyful thoughts. Meditate to train your mind. Savor the present moment; it is where you can return after your body dies. When you are on the other side, you can relive any moment you lived. But you can only fully relive moments you were fully present for. Each moment you are aware of, in the NOW, you can recall after your body dies. This is true currency.

Balance is important too. A physical lifetime brings many joys that can only be savored properly in a physical body. These physical experiences are also spiritual experiences when you are aware of the present moment.

You add each of these present moments to your collective wisdom. This wisdom, you have the best access to after your body dies, but you can access your soul's wisdom, right now. No need to arrange and untimely death!

You can access your higher wisdom through meditation. When you meditate, you are able to contact and connect with your Higher Mind. You are able to retrieve memories from every lifetime you have ever lived. And you can bring that innate wisdom forward to enhance and inform your lives now.

Your soul is tremendously wise. Your soul is able to retrieve solutions to problems before you even need it fixed. Meditation accesses this deep wisdom easily and with the least effort.

You are doing a great job! Even tiny steps towards greater ease brings huge changes to the world and the universe. Your self-development work truly helps every living (and non-living!) soul.

Don't be too hard on yourself for not meeting your own self-imposed standards of behaviour. We make no such judgments. We are only interested and supportive of your best interest in every moment. Shame and self-flagellation are never helpful. Forgive yourself and move on.

From our perspective, it is not needed to forgive you, because we see the Whole. Just be gentle with yourself. Be gentle with others, for they are mirrors of the self.

Make your NOW moment the best you are able.

Let go of anger today. NOW.

Let go of worry today. NOW.

Be grateful today. NOW.

Do your work today. NOW.

Be kind to every living thing, including yourself, today. NOW.

Do this and happiness will cling closer to you than your own shadow. Always there. Always yours. Without question.

All blessings are yours.
All my blessings upon you.
All is forever well.

Namaste,
Mikao Usui.

APPENDIX:

Affirmation Ladders

Start where you are! Work your way up to a set of strongly positive affirmations by a series of little steps. Just as you would climb a ladder only step by step, you can practice affirmations in the same way. Gradually, your mood, outlook, and point of manifestation will shift toward the positive.

You will rate your level of anger, worry, gratitude, meditative work, and kindness, the five Reiki Ideals, on a scale of 0 to 10. Zero being none and ten being a lot! For anger and worry, the goal is to decrease the levels to zero. For gratitude, meditative work, and kindness, the goal is to increase the levels to 10.

These affirmation ladders are a tool for change! They are not meant as a system of ranking or comparing. These affirmations are just for YOU. Don't give them to your mother, brother, or lover. Do your OWN work. Leave others alone!

To get the most out of these affirmations, you will be honestly acknowledging where you are. There is no need to judge yourself harshly or beat yourself up for not being where you think you should be. Just be gentle with yourself, practice the affirmation at the level you are at, and over time, you will nudge up one step and another, until you are feeling true, deep, happiness and joy.

Mini Practise

Commitment time for this activity is less than 5 minutes.
Start at the level you are at NOW for each Reiki Ideal. Read **upwards** through each Affirmation Ladder, just letting the words wash over you. Imagine what it would feel like if the statements at the top of the page were true for you.

Quick Practise

Commitment time for this activity 10 to 15 minutes
For a quick practice, check in with your current level of anger, worry, gratitude, meditative work, and kindness on a scale of zero to ten. Read the affirmation you are at for each of the Ideals. Say each affirmation out loud ten times each. The affirmations themselves will nudge you to the next level, while also acknowledging the truth of where you are at now. There is no burying or suppressing emotions here! Just an honest appraisal and a gentle releasing of thoughts and emotions that are no longer serving you.

Longer Practice

Commitment time for this activity is 30 to 45 minutes.
If you have longer and are serious about changing your life and getting happy, once and for all, rate each Reiki Ideal three times. In between each rating, say the affirmation out loud 10 times, while looking in the mirror.

Letting Go of Anger

Begin by rating the level of anger in your body-mind, right now. Scan your body and look for tension or ease. Feel the truth for you in this moment. Rank your anger on a scale from 0 to 10. Zero is a feeling of being completely happy and at peace; ten is feeling blind rage, as angry as you ever have ever felt in your life, literally howling with rage. Close your eyes, don't over think it, and pick the first number that pops into your head

Repeat the affirmation at least ten times for the number you are at now. Look in a mirror and pay attention to how you feel as you repeat it. Does it feel true for you? Be willing to go up or down a number to get a greater ease in your body. It is okay; just be honest.

Scan your body again from head to toe. Scan your heart and your mind. Feel what is true for you, NOW. Take a deep breath, close your eyes, and rate your level of anger again. Did it change? Go up? Go down? Stay the same? All of these results are perfectly fine. Go to the affirmation for the level you are NOW at and repeat it 10 times, while looking in your eyes. Try it now.

Scan your body-mind a third time and rate your anger level. Practice the affirmation for the level you are honestly at (it really is okay if it goes up, down, or stays the same!). Even if you are not yet at the top, at zero, that is okay! Just being **willing** to shift your experience is enough to start the changes.

Letting Go of Anger Affirmation Ladder

0	Peace becomes me. I am peaceful, joyful, and loving. I understand my true nature is joy.
1	Love is everywhere I look. It is all around me all the time.
2	Love, peace and understanding are always available to me. Each breath I breathe is a new chance.
3	Peace is all around me, right around the corner. I know where to look to find the answers I need.
4	Breathing in, I am love. Breathing out, I have time. Every breath offers me a chance to change.
5	I take the time to know myself. I know that I am loving and lovable.
6	I embrace my feelings with love and acceptance. I know I can sort out the real issue below it all.
7	All my emotions are wise teachers. I accept them as the lessons they are. Clarity is all around me.
8	I am feeling angry and it is okay. I know I can use the energy released by this angry experience for positive change.
9	I am feeling angry. Although I am angry right now, I know this feeling will pass and I will get clarity on the real issue.
10	I am feeling really angry right now. Absolutely furious. Even though I am so overcome with anger and rage right now, I am still a good person.

Letting Go of Worry

Just as with anger, rate your current level of worry on a scale from 0 to 10. Ten is being completely frozen and consumed by fear, worry, and anxiety to the point where you are not able to function. Zero is feeling wonderful, optimistic, joyful, and safe. Take a deep breath; scan your body-mind. Close your eyes and rank your current level of worry.

Practice the affirmation for the level of worry you are at right NOW. Look in a mirror; say the affirmation out loud at least 10 times.

Scan your body-mind again and rate your worry a second time. It is perfectly fine to go up, go down, or stay the same. Be honest. Be gentle. Practice the new affirmation (or the same one) 10 times, while looking in your own eyes.

Great job! Keep going! Scan again. Rate your worry from 0 to 10. Practice the affirmation for the level of worry you are at NOW. Ten times, looking into your gorgeous eyes. The changes are happening. You are doing so well!

Letting Go of Worry Affirmation Ladder

0	Things always work out for me. I trust in Divine solutions.
1	I know I am always safe and loved. The Divine is on my side.
2	I believe in me. God/the Divine/the Universe does too.
3	My wise-self guides me to the best outcome. I listen to the voice of my soul.
4	I can see many possibilities. There are many options available to me now.
5	I am safe to grow and to change. I accept my human mistakes as a chance to grow and change. It is okay to be human!
6	I accept this situation for what it is. I allow life to be as it is.
7	Breathing in, I am here. Breathing out, it is now.
8	Even though I am really worried about this, I am willing to accept and love myself just as I am.
9	I am gripped with worry right now. It feels awful to be in this place, but I can take one tiny action right now to change. Just one tiny breath to let in freedom.
10	I am terrified and completely frozen by worry right now. Even though worry dominates my thoughts, I am still able to breathe. If I am still breathing, I still have a chance.

Being Grateful

Now rate your level of gratitude on a scale from 0 to 10. Zero is feeling critical and depressed; **nothing** is good in your life. Ten is feeling that you are overflowing with joy, gratitude, and appreciation; your heart is so full with all your blessings. Honour what is happening for you right now. Honestly assess your gratitude, without fear or judgment. There is no right or wrong here. Just start where you are, knowing your feelings can all shift in a moment. Take a deep breath. Close your eyes. Rate your gratitude level right now.

Practice the gratitude affirmation for the level you are at NOW, at least 10 times.

Breathe deeply. Close your eyes. Scan your body-mind. Now, rate your level of gratitude once more. Practice the new affirmation (or the same one) 10 times, while looking in your own eyes. Great work!

Now, scan once more. Check in with your heart. How full is your heart with gratitude? It is okay if it is still next to empty. That just means you are depleted and in need of some self-care. Hey! I know some awesome self-care, Affirmations! Tune in to the number you are at now. Take the new affirmation around the mental track ten times for a test drive.

Breathe again. Rate your level. Be gentle. Repeat the affirmation for the new level ten times. Give yourself a high five.

Gratitude Affirmation Ladder

10	I am tremendously grateful for all my many experiences. Life grows and expands through me! I love my life!
9	I am filled with appreciation for every aspect of my life. I am so lucky to be me!
8	I love my life. I appreciate all I have and all I am able to give. I am generous and abundant in my gratitude.
7	I am so grateful for my life, the good and the bad. I am so grateful for all my teachers, the good and the bad. Everyone is my teacher; I honour them for these lessons.
6	I appreciate my many blessings. Everywhere I look, I see love surrounding me. My gratitude increases what I see.
5	My life is getting better every day. I see miracles every time I look. I appreciate the gifts and challenges of life now.
4	The Ground below my feet, the Air above my head, these two Powers help me in so many ways every day. Thank you Earth. Thank you Sky.
3	I appreciate my ability to breathe, to read, to learn, to live. I am alive. There is hope.
2	I acknowledge the tiny glimmer of hope in the darkness. Day follows night; night follows day. I look to Nature's cycles as evidence that hope is possible.
1	My life is in crisis right now. Even though my life is currently a mess, I can acknowledge that I am alive, I can breathe, my heart is still beating.
0	My life is in chaos right now. Nothing seems to be going right for me at the moment. Even though everything is going so badly right now, I am still a good person.

Do Your Work

So are you seeing the pattern? Breathe, Rate, Affirm, Repeat. Like shampoo bottle instructions, but better. It could be easy to slide into "supposed to" self-shaming when checking in with how often you are currently meditating. I would like you to consider this first; shame keeps us from doing positive actions for our own well-being. Resist the urge to tell yourself you are bad. You are good. You are grand. You have gotten this far. You ARE doing the work. Honour what you are able to accomplish; let go of the expectations. Remember, you meditate the moment you breathe consciously. See! You are probably meditating right now!

Rate your current level of doing the work, meditating, doing self care, nourishing your soul, from 0 to 10. Zero being you do not meditate or do any self-care at all — at its core, this is caused by a feeling of unworthiness — and ten being you are immersed in mindfulness and inner stillness.

Now, go ahead, check in with your affirmations. Breathe and repeat the cycle *two* more times. Then give yourself another hug and congratulations for doing some great work today.

Do your Work Affirmation Ladder

10	Now... I am here. Every moment is a meditation.
9	I allow all good to flow to me now. I surrender to the stillness of the soul.
8	I am filled with light and with life in every breath I breathe.
7	Everywhere I go, everywhere I look, I see opportunities to connect and expand.
6	Expansion, Joy, and Peace are in each breath.
5	I honour myself and my worth. I meditate.
4	Breathing in, I am enough. Breathing out, I am worthy.
3	I am only a moment away from connecting to my Source. It doesn't take much time, just one deep breath.
2	I honour where I am right now. I breathe in knowing; I breathe out resistance.
1	I am willing to release the need to put myself last.
0	Right now, I do not feel worthy of Divine Love or self-care. But I can change all that with one deep breath.

Being Kind

Do you know how amazing you are? You are. Really. Amazing. That is you. Your willingness to even consider this affirmation work, much less do any of it, is truly amazing. High fives!

Now, for the last Affirmation Ladder as part of the Reiki Ideals, kindness! How kind are you being with yourself right now? How kind are you being with others right now? Again, no need to go into condemnation or self-shaming; that will just set you backward. Just take a deep breath. Rate your level of kindness to yourself and others on a scale from 0 to 10. Ten is feeling and acting completely kind to every living thing, including yourself. Zero is feeling and acting with hate and cruelty toward yourself or another.

Be easy about this. It is okay to be wherever you are. Know that you can be honest here, because you are able to change. So where are you at, right now, with kindness?

Practise the corresponding kindness affirmation ten times. Breathe again. Hug yourself again. Smile into your eyes. Now, rate your kindness level a second time. Practise a second round of kindness affirmations for the level you are NOW at, ten times each. Good. Awesome job. Last one. Check in with your body-mind. Rate your kindness level one last time. Practise the affirmation for the level you are at NOW. You are awesome!

Kindness Affirmation Ladder

10	Kindness within me. Kindness all around me. I am kind and loving.
9	I love myself the way I am. I am kind and gentle.
8	I love myself; therefore, I am kind. I am kind; therefore, I am love.
7	I am kind and gentle with me. I am kind and gentle with others.
6	The soft breath of kindness enters my heart. I allow kindness to be my way.
5	Each moment, I am kind. Each moment I breathe, I am kind. Every moment I begin again.
4	I'm giving myself a break. I'm cutting myself some slack. I'm choosing kindness and peace over suffering and self-punishment.
3	I ask now for the courage to find kindness in my heart. God/Divine/Goddess, please help me.
2	Each moment, day by day, I make reparations and amends for my past behaviour. Each moment is a new moment. I can choose peace.
1	Unkind thoughts and words have been my pattern, but I can change. I can choose to be kind.
0	I have been cruel and mean to myself or others. Even though my behaviour was wrong, I can choose differently, starting now. I am still a good person.

Epilogue

Writing this book changed me. I suppose that could be said of any book and author. But I am different at the end of this book than I was at the start.

I am more. I am more ME. I am more me than I have ever given myself permission to be. Lately, I wake up and check to see if I still have permission to be unreasonably happy.

So far, it has been a YES every day.

My happiness is unreasonable, because it is not connected to outer events. It is generated from within, like a light in a lighthouse. And just like that light, happiness is reflected off everything I am near.

The optical illusion of a light like that is it could appear as though the happiness is 'out there', where I see its warm glow shining. But always, always, the light of happiness only exists within me.

It has to be tended, like a hearth fire. It has to be nurtured, so it doesn't go out. But that light of happiness always originates from the inside out.

My hope is that this book helped you build your own bright light of happiness. My wish is that you also see this warm glow of reflected light all around you, every day. It was within you all along.

Acknowledgements

This book would not have been possible without the help of many, many people.

In humble gratitude, I thank: Kim Johnston, Michael Breithaupt, Tarra Riley, and Jevon Hills, my first ever Reiki peeps. My best teachers.

My love and gratitude to Samantha Baldwin and her amazing family in the 'Baldwin Big Top'. Thank you for encouraging me to keep writing and listening to first drafts and my occasional writerly meltdowns. You are my she-ro!

Thank you to all of the people who read and provided early comments on my first chapter: Laura Lamont, Michelle Bastock, Oksana Porteous, Kait Frank, Rita Reddy, and Parisa Radmanesh You gave me the courage to keep going!

To all my darling extended families (on all the sides!) and wonderful, uplifting friends. I am so very grateful you are in my life!

Thank you to all my Reiki Students! You guys inspire me so much! Thank you for teaching me how important it is for me to get over my nerves and share this work with a bigger audience. If one person is helped by this book, it is because of you.

And of course, always, my deep love and appreciation to Christopher Calon, my husband, and our darling son, Zane. You two are the glue. You keep me together! Thank you for putting up with me completely ignoring you while I wrote. Thank you for bugging me to put down the pen, step away from the laptop, and have some fun. Thank you for all the trips out to the mountains, on a whim, just to enjoy each other's company. Thank you for reminding me, again and again, why I do this work. I love you!

⇉ About Geneva Robins ⇇

Geneva is a Reiki Master, wife, mother, scientist, scholar, and basically a student of Divine Wisdom wherever she can find it. She reads continually on how to improve the spirit-mind-body connection and then discovers that it is all perfect and surrenders it all to the Divine, sits back, and watches miracles happen.

She studied ecology as part of her formal academic training, which gave her the much needed stamina and perseverance that she would need to build her second career in helping people connect to their Divine-selves.

She sees patterns in the chaos and she sees chaos underlying too much order. She is a student of the Tao Te Ching, the Gnostic Gospels, the Dhammapada, and, of course, Reiki.

She completed her Reiki courses in 2007, but she is a perpetual student of Reiki itself. Her curiosity into the nature of reality and how Reiki fits into it all is a lifetime course she happily takes every day.

She lives in Calgary, Alberta, Canada, in between the trees of the Rocky Mountains and the dinosaurs of the Badlands. She loves walking in nature with her husband and son, sipping tea with her friends, and wandering through bookstores and coffee shops.

She owns too many books.

Connect with Geneva at genevarobins.com. She loves cheering you on as you travel on your own journey to realize it is all perfect. Email your questions, testimonials, or realizations to geneva@genevarobins.com.

Made in the
USA
Columbia, SC